Recycling Recipes

Institute of Scrap Iron and Steel, Inc.

The Institute of Scrap Iron and Steel, founded in 1928, is a national association headquartered in Washington, D.C. The more than 1,600 member companies process about 95 percent of all scrap purchased in the U.S. or exported.

In commemoration of its 50th anniversary, the Institute commissioned world renowned artist Mark di Suvero to create a monumental sculpture as a gift to the people of America.

Made from iron and steel scrap, and weighing 30 tons, "Isis" was dedicated on July 19, 1978 at the Smithsonian Institution's Hirshhorn Museum and Sculpture Garden in Washington, D.C. where it is on permanent display.

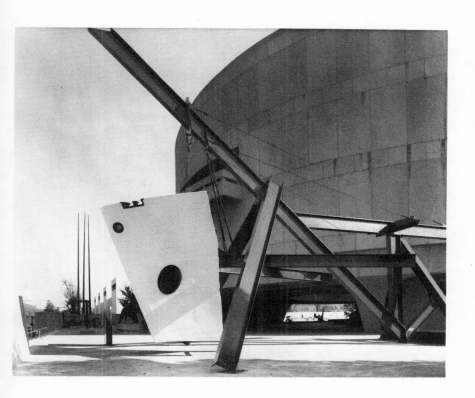

ACKNOWLEDGEMENT

"Recycling Recipes with Members of ISIS" is the collection of recipes submitted for the Institute sponsored *My Favorite Recipe Contest* which was held in conjunction with the 1981 Convention.

National Officers

President
MORTON B. PLANT
H. Klaff & Co., Inc.
Division of Steelmet, Inc.
Baltimore, Maryland

First Vice President
JAMES F. ANDERTON
Summit Steel Processing Corp.
Lansing, Michigan

Second Vice President
STEVEN KAPLAN
M.S. Kaplan Co.
Chicago, Illinois

Treasurer
JACK BECK
Western Iron & Metal Co.
Milwaukee, Wisconsin

Secretary
DAVID S. BLUE
Louisville Scrap Material Co., Inc.
Louisville, Kentucky

The Institute wishes to thank the chefs of Caesars Palace, Las Vegas, Nevada, who judged the contest and the owners of Jarvis Kitchenware, Washington, D.C., for their guidance in the preparation of this publication.

TABLE OF CONTENTS

A PRACTICAL GUIDE TO WEIGHTS AND MEASURES

1 tablespoon = 3 teaspoons
1 teaspoon = ⅓ tablespoon
2 tablespoons = ⅛ cup (1 ounce)
4 tablespoons = ¼ cup
5⅓ tablespoons = ⅓ cup
8 tablespoons = ½ cup
16 tablespoons = 1 cup
⅜ cup = 6 tablespoons
⅝ cup = 10 tablespoons
1 cup = ½ pint
2 cups = 1 pint
2 pints = 1 quart
4 quarts = 1 gallon
8 quarts = 1 peck
4 pecks = 1 bushel
1 pound = 16 ounces
1 fluid ounce = 2 tablespoons
16 fluid ounces = 1 pint
1 liter = 2 pints = 1 quart
6 ounce can = 6 ounces = ¾ cup
8 ounce can = 8 ounces = 1 cup
#1 can = 11 ounces = 1⅓ cups
#303 can = 16 ounces = 2 cups
#2 can = 20 ounces = 2½ cups
#2½ can = 28 ounces = 3½ cups

Appetizers
and
Hors d'Oeuvres

MOCK CRAB FONDUE

Preparation Time: 30 minutes
Cooking Time: 15 minutes

Serves: 20
Prepare Ahead
Freeze

2 lbs. halibut steak
1 lb. Old English cheese
2 tsp. milk
½ c. Haute Sautern Wine

1 pkg. large sesame seed
crackers (or crackers of
your choice)

Add halibut to 4 quarts rapidly boiling water. Immediately turn off heat. Allow halibut to "poach" for 15 minutes. Drain. In the meantime melt cheese together with milk in a 2 quart fondue pot. Remove from heat, add wine and flaked halibut. (More wine may be required after standing.)

Serve hot with crackers.

"Excellent for the person allergic to crab."

Janice Carnes (Mrs. Earl L.)
D & J Press Company, Inc.
North Tonawanda, New York

HOT CRAB DIP

Preparation Time: 10 minutes
Cooking Time: 30-45 minutes
Oven Temperature: 350°

Serves: 4-6
servings
Prepare Ahead

1 can crab meat
2 3 oz. pkgs. cream
cheese
¼ c. half & half
¼ c. mayonnaise
2 drops Tabasco
½-1 tsp. Worcestershire
(to taste)

1-2 tbsp. sherry
1 tsp. dried onion
½ garlic clove, pressed
1 tsp. chopped chives
salt
pepper

Soften cream cheese. Mix all ingredients together adding more seasonings to taste if needed. Bake in 350° oven for 30-45 minutes.

Serve with Bremner crackers.

"Very easy and quick with a fantastic taste."

Nancy Grafrath (Mrs. S. L.)
S. R. Robinson & Co.
Chicago, Illinois

DILL SEED DIP

Preparation Time: 30 minutes
Prepare Ahead

Serves: 30 (single recipe serves 15 people)

⅔ c. sour cream
⅔ c. mayonnaise
2 tbsp. onion flakes or
** 3 tbsp. fresh chopped onion**

2 tbsp. parsley
2 tsp. dill seed or
** 2 tbsp. fresh dill**
2 tsp. Beau Monde seasoning

Mix all of the above ingredients together and refrigerate. Buy an oval braided challah bread or a round dark pumpernickel bread. Slice off top 1 inch of bread. Scoop out the soft inside of the bread, leaving a 1 inch wall. Fill with dip and use scooped out bread cut in chunks for dipping.

Double the recipe to fill bread.

"An attractive and tasty centerpiece."

Sharon Loef (Mrs. Frederick)
The Loef Co., Inc.
Athens, Georgia

9

SHRIMP DIP

Preparation Time: 15 minutes   *Serves: 25*
Prepare Ahead

½ lb. cooked shrimp
3 tbsp. chili sauce
½ tsp. lemon juice
4 tbsp. milk

1 8 oz. pkg. cream cheese
4 tsp. onion juice
¼ tsp. Worcestershire sauce

Finely chop shrimp or leave whole if they are very small. Cream the cheese and add chili sauce, onion juice, lemon juice, Worcestershire sauce and shrimp. Gradually beat in enough milk to give a good dipping consistency. Makes about 2½ cups. You can use more shrimp and a little garlic.

"Serve with crackers or chips and your favorite cocktail."

Barbara Glick (Mrs. Howard)
Tri-State Iron & Metal Co.
Texarkana, Texas

HEARTY CHILI DIP

Preparation Time: 15 minutes   *Serves: 12 or*
Cooking Time: 15 minutes   *more*
                                                      Prepare Ahead
                                                      Freeze

1 lb. of hamburger
1 can chili (no beans)

1 lb. Velveeta cheese

Brown hamburger; drain grease; add chili with no beans and cubed Velveeta cheese. Heat slowly until all cheese is melted and hot. (Microwave is excellent for heating mixture.) Serve with Fritos or Corn Chips.

"Quick, hearty dip which most men and teenagers enjoy."

Dorothy Ransom (Mrs. Garland)
Missouri Rolling Mill
St. Louis, Missouri

SEAFOOD AND JULIENNED VEGETABLES IN CREAM SAUCE

Preparation Time: 30 minutes
Cooking Time: 30-35 minutes

Serves: 6
Prepare Ahead

1 whole lobster (1½ lbs.)
12 medium shrimp
8 fresh sea scallops
4 c. dry white wine
1 c. water
2 tbsp. raspberry vinegar
1 bouquet garni
1 small carrot, finely julienned

1 small zucchini, finely julienned
1 small leek, finely julienned
1⅓ c. heavy cream
salt and white pepper
freshly chopped parsley for garnish

Remove lobster and shrimp from shells. Cut lobster into pieces and devein and butterfly shrimp. Slice scallops, set seafood aside. Reserve shells for stock. In 4 qt. saucepan bring wine, water and vinegar to boil. Add a bouquet garni and reserved shells to liquid and simmer 25 minutes. Strain stock through several layers of cheesecloth into another pot and return to simmer. Add seafood and simmer for 3 minutes. Add julienned vegetables and continue to simmer until seafood is done and vegetables are crisp tender, approximately 2 minutes. Stir in heavy cream and heat but do not boil. Salt and pepper to taste. Ladle into soup bowls and garnish with parsley.

"Assorted seafood and vegetables in a light cream sauce."

Sharon Naporano
(Mrs. Andrew J.)
Naporano Iron & Metal Co.
Newark, New Jersey

MUSSELS SAN LAURE

Preparation Time: 20 minutes   *Serves: 6*
Cooking Time: 1 hour plus   *Prepare ahead*

4 doz. Mussels*	1 tsp. basil
2 c. water	1 tsp. finely chopped garlic
4 tbsp. butter (divided usage)	½ tsp. tarragon
	½ tsp. oregano
3 tbsp. flour	¼ c. sherry
1 c. chopped tomatoes	2 Italian bread loaves
1 c. chopped mushrooms	peanut oil
3 tbsp. dill	3 tbsp. Parmesan cheese
1 bay leaf	

Scrub the mussels thoroughly. In a pot bring to boil 2 cups water. Drop in the mussels, cover and boil over high heat checking to determine the precise moment when the mussels have opened. Remove the mussels at once, separate the mussel from the shell and reserve the mussel. Boil the liquid down to two cups and strain stock through cheesecloth twice in order to remove all sand and grit. Reserve stock.

Melt 2 tablespoons butter over low heat. Blend in 3 tablespoons flour and cook slowly for about 2 mintues not allowing the mixture to brown. Remove from heat and blend in the two cups of strained mussel stock. Return to high heat for about one minute, stirring constantly to allow sauce to thicken.

Saute in 2 tablespoons butter, tomatoes, mushrooms, dill, bay leaf, basil, garlic, tarragon and oregano.

Combine the mussel sauce with the tomato mixture and add sherry.

Cut the bread loaf into slices 1½" thick, hollow out center of bread, leaving ¼" layer of bread on bottom. Deep fry the hollowed out bread pieces in peanut oil until crispy. Drain well.

When ready to serve, add grated Parmesan cheese and the mussels to the sauce, heat thoroughly and pour over the breads.
*In lieu of fresh mussels you can used canned ones. If the reserved juice from the cans doesn't equal 2 cups add clam juice or water or white wine to bring the liquid to the two cups.

"Mussels prepared with tomatoes and herbs served in French bread boats."

Connie and Sandy Shapiro
Cambridge Iron & Metal Co.
Baltimore, Maryland

FRESH SALMON APPETIZER

Preparation Time: 30-40 minutes
Cooking Time: 40 minutes

Prepare Ahead
Freeze (is better fresh)

2 lbs. fresh red sockeye salmon fillets with skin removed
1 12 oz. jar bread & butter pickles (with juice)

1 12 oz. bottle Heinz catsup
2 medium Spanish onions, sliced in rings
1 tbsp. vinegar

Bring pickles, catsup and vinegar to a fast boil; add onions. Boil at a slow simmer ½ hour. Cut raw fish in approximately 1 inch cubes. (Not too small.) Check very carefully to remove all bones. When pickle mixture has finished cooking for ½ hour, add salmon and fast boil 2-5 minutes until salmon is cooked through. Refrigerate and serve well chilled!

"Serve warm as a luncheon entree."

Carol Leach
Mandak Metals Processors
Selkirk, Manitoba, Canada

13

SALMON TARTARE

Preparation Time: 45 minutes

Serves: 6 to 8
Prepare Ahead

3 lbs. uncooked, deboned
  salmon
1 large onion, coarsely
  chopped
2 to 3 garlic cloves,
  minced
salt, pepper—to taste
lemon juice—to taste
  (liberal)

1 tbsp. Dijon mustard
chopped parsley—to taste
2 tbsp. dill
brandy—to taste (1 to 2
  tbsp.)
sliced green olives
melba toast

Add onion and garlic to coarsely chopped salmon; add salt, pepper, lemon juice, mustard, parsley, dill and brandy to taste. Mold into fish or oval shape. Garnish with sliced olives and extra parsley. Serve with melba toast.

"A real conversation piece."

Ruth L. Fox (Mrs. Robert)
Markowitz & Fox
San Jose, California

ARTICHOKE NIBBLES I

Preparation Time: 30 minutes
Cooking Time: 30 minutes
Oven Temperature: 325°

Serves: 6 to 8
Prepare Ahead
Freeze

2 jars (6 oz. ea.) marinated
  artichoke hearts
1 small onion, finely
  chopped
1 clove garlic, minced or
  mashed
4 eggs
¼ c. fine dry bread
  crumbs

¼ tsp. salt
⅛ tsp. each—pepper,
  oregano, liquid hot pepper
½ lb. sharp cheddar cheese,
  shredded (2 c.)
2 tsp. minced parsley

14

Drain marinade from 1 jar of artichokes into a frying pan. Drain the other jar, do not reserve liquid. Chop artichokes, set aside. Add onion and garlic to frying pan; saute until onions are soft. Beat eggs; add bread crumbs, salt, pepper, oregano, and hot pepper. Stir in cheese, parsley, artichokes and sauteed onion mixture. Turn into greased 7" x 11" baking pan or dish. Bake at 325° for 30 minutes. Cook and cut into 1" squares. Serve cold or hot.

"Tasty little squares easy to prepare. I prefer them warm."

Kate Hightower (Mrs. William)
Ferromet Inc.
Upland, California

ARTICHOKE NIBBLES II

Preparation Time: 50 minutes
Cooking Time: 35 minutes
Oven Temperature: 325°

Serves: 6 to 8
Prepare Ahead
Freeze

1 can or jar artichokes
½ c. bread crumbs
4 eggs
1 small onion, chopped
¼ tsp. oregano

1 tbsp. minced garlic
3 dashes hot pepper sauce
3 c. shredded cheddar
cheese

Chop artichokes and onion. Add oregano, garlic and hot pepper sauce. In separate bowl beat eggs; add bread crumbs and cheese. Add artichoke mixture to egg mixture. Place in oblong baking dish approximately 8" x 12" or 2 quarts. Bake at 325° for 35 minutes. Cut in squares and serve hot or cold.

"Tasty accompaniment to drinks."

Esther Shiff (Mrs. Jay)
Fostoria Iron and Metal Co.
Fostoria, Ohio

ARTICHOKE SURPRISE

Preparation Time: 20 minutes
Cooking Time: Broil 1-3 minutes

Serves: 24 pieces
Prepare Ahead
Freeze

1 14 oz. can of artichoke
hearts
6 pieces of white or egg
bread, toasted

1 c. mayonnaise
1 c. grated Parmesan cheese
paprika

First toast 6 pieces white or egg bread. Cut off crust and cut each piece in 4 squares. Mix mayonnaise and Parmesan cheese, set aside. Cut each artichoke heart in four. Put one piece on top of each piece of toast. Put a spoonful of cheese-mayo mixture on top of each artichoke heart, to cover. Sprinkle with paprika. Place under broiler until topping melts (1-3 minutes).

"Delicious even for non-artichoke eaters."

Debra Grossman
Grossman Bros. Company
Milwaukee, Wisconsin

CANTONESE MEATBALLS

Serves: 30 meatballs   *Freeze*
Prepare Ahead

Meatballs
1 lb. ground beef
1¼ tsp. ground ginger
½ c. water
1 tsp. salt to taste
1 tbsp. chili sauce
½ tsp. A-1 sauce
¼ c. Matzo meal or bread
   crumbs
1 egg
1 small onion, grated
¼ tsp. black pepper

Cantonese Sauce
¼ c. brown sugar, packed
   firmly
½ tsp. ground ginger
¼ tsp. salt
2 tbsp. cornstarch
1 1 lb. 4½ oz. can pineapple
   chunks
1 c. pineapple juice
¼ c. vinegar
2 tbsp. soy sauce
1 green pepper cut into thin
   strips
1 c. thinly sliced celery
sweet pickles, sliced
1 peeled tomato cut into
   wedges (optional)

Meatballs   Mix together all ingredients with exception of onion. Make mixture into small meat balls (the size of large walnuts). Brown in 1 tbsp. hot oil. Remove to another pot. Add onion and a little water to meatballs and simmer for about an hour, then drain and add cantonese sauce.

Cantonese Sauce   Mix sugar, ginger, salt, and cornstarch together, add juice, vinegar and soy sauce to dry ingredients; blend until smooth. Cook until slightly thickened; stirring constantly. Add green bell pepper slices, celery, a few pieces of mixed sweet pickles, then pour over drained meat balls. Cover and simmer 10 minutes. Cut pineapple into chunks or use chunks and add with tomatoes to meat balls and sauce. Cover and simmer 10 more minutes. Do not double sauce recipe.

"Also makes a delicious entree to be served with rice."
Sarah Loef (Mrs. Harry)
The Loef Co., Inc.
Athens, Georgia

SWEDISH MEATBALLS

Preparation Time: 30 minutes
Cooking Time: 30 minutes

Serves: 12-15
Prepare Ahead

1½ c. soft bread crumbs
3 tbsp. onion, chopped
   fine
5 tbsp. butter
1½ tsp. salt
1 lb. ground beef
¾ c. milk

¼ tsp. nutmeg (do not omit)
1 egg slightly beaten
⅛ tsp. pepper
1 10½ oz. can beef
   consomme
1½ tbsp. flour
1½ tbsp. water

Saute chopped onion in half the butter for 5 minutes. Add to bread crumbs; then add beef, nutmeg, salt, pepper, egg and milk. Mix well and form into 1 inch balls. Saute in remaining butter until browned. Add consomme, cover and simmer five minutes. Remove meat to heated serving dish. Blend flour and water and add to consomme. Stir until smooth and thickened, then pour over meatballs. (If prepared several hours in advance, add meatballs to thickened gravy and keep warm until serving time.)

"An easy, economical, elegant appetizer with unique flavor."

Jane A. Fulton (Mrs. Edwin O.)
Fulton Supply and
   Recycling, Inc.
Denton, Texas

CAVIAR & EGGS

Preparation Time: 15 minutes
Serves: 15-20

Prepare Ahead
(The morning
of the party)

1 doz. medium eggs, (hard
   boiled & chopped)
1 medium onion, chopped
   fine
¼ lb. butter, melted

2 2 oz. jars of black
   whitefish caviar
1 pt. sour cream
chopped parsley (optional)
party rye

18

Combine chopped eggs, chopped onion and melted butter. Line pie plate with egg mixture as you would crumbs for crust, patting bottom and sides. Fill center with pint of sour cream. Place in freezer (covered) for 2 hours. Remove from freezer and spread caviar across top. Can be decorated around side with chopped parsley. Put in refrigerator until ready to serve with party rye.

"Easy party fare!"

Leatrie Kramer (Mrs. Sidney)
I. Kramer & Sons, Inc.
Greenfield, Massachusetts

SHRIMP COCKTAIL SPREAD

Preparation Time: 15 minutes

Serves: 25
Prepare Ahead

1 8 oz. pkg. cream cheese
1 c. cocktail sauce (or 1 c. catsup & 1 tbsp. horseradish)

1 7 oz. can salad shrimp
lemon wedges & parsley to garnish

Spread softened cream cheese onto a dinner plate as if frosting a cake. Cover entire plate. Spread cocktail sauce on top of cream cheese. Place rinsed, drained shrimp on top of the sauce. Garnish with lemon wedges and parsley for color. Resembles a pizza when finished and is eaten on crackers. Use knife for serving and spreading on crackers.

"Easy, colorful, and different cracker spread for shrimp lovers."

Gay A. Wynveen
Miller Compressing Company
Milwaukee, Wisconsin

CAPONATA
(ITALIAN EGGPLANT APPETIZER)

Preparation Time: 1 hour　　　　　　　*Prepare Ahead*
Cooking Time: 45 minutes

1 lb. eggplant (peeled and cubed ½" cubes)
¼ to ½ c. olive oil
1 c. finely chopped celery
1 small onion, finely chopped
2 tbsp. wine vinegar mixed with 4 tsp. sugar

1 1 lb. can Italian plum tomatoes (drain and reserve liquid)
4 tbsp. tomato paste
1 5 oz. jar stuffed green olives
1 small can whole mushrooms
salt & pepper to taste

Sprinkle cubes of eggplant with salt and set on paper towels to drain. After 30 minutes pat dry. Meanwhile, in a heavy skillet heat ¼ cup oil. Add celery and onions, cook 10 minutes (until celery and onions are soft and lightly colored). Transfer (with slotted spoon) to a bowl. Add remaining oil and saute eggplant over high heat, stirring and turning constantly for 8 to 10 minutes (until lightly browned). Return celery, onion and add other ingredients. Bring to boil; reduce heat and simmer uncovered stirring frequently for 15 minutes. Chill well before serving. Serve on crackers or thin sliced French bread.

Mrs. L. G. Galamba
S. G. Metal Industries
Kansas City, Kansas

PARTY CRAB SPREAD

Preparation Time: 45 minutes   *Serves: 16-20*
Cooking Time: 5-10 minutes   *Prepare Ahead*

1½ tbsp. plain gelatin
¼ c. cold water
1 can condensed cream of
  mushroom soup
1 c. mayonnaise
1 tbsp. Worcestershire
  sauce
1 small onion, minced

1 8 oz. pkg. cream cheese
½ tsp. salt
2 cans (7½ oz. ea.)
  crabmeat, flaked (or
  equivalent of fresh or
  frozen)
1 c. finely chopped celery

Soften gelatin in cold water. Heat soup, mayonnaise, Worcestershire, onion, and cream cheese in top of double boiler until cheese is melted. Add gelatin and salt; stir until dissolved. Chill until partly set; fold in crabmeat and celery. Turn into a 1½ qt. mold. Chill until firm. Serve with Ritz crackers. (I use a round mold, fill center with parsley and surround with Ritz crackers on a round serving platter.)

"A delicious creamy crabmeat hors d'oeuvre."

Bobbie Strum
Atlas Metal & Iron Corp.
Chicago, Illinois

CHILI AND RELLENOS SOUFFLE OLE

Preparation Time: 15 minutes   *Serves: 6*
Cooking Time: 45 to 60 minutes   *Prepare Ahead*
Oven Temperature: 350°

1 7 oz. can green chilies,   **1½ c. milk**
   drained and diced   **4 eggs, beaten**
6 oz. sharp cheddar   **¼ c. flour**
   cheese (grated—1½ c.)   **½ tsp. salt**

Mix together diced chilies and cheese. Put in a souffle dish or 8" square casserole. Combine remaining ingredients and beat until smooth. Pour over the chilies and cheese. Bake in 350° oven for 45 to 60 minutes. (Test with toothpick. If it comes out clean, souffle is done.) Serve with chunky type taco sauce.

"Mexican recipe—with a zing and yet—very tasty—simple and different."

> **Beverlee M. Klein**
> **Key Metals, Inc.**
> **Santa Ana, California**

ZUCCHINI QUICHE

Preparation Time: 20-25 minutes   *Serves: 6-8*
Cooking Time: 30-40 minutes   *Prepare Ahead*
Oven temperature: 350°   *Freeze*

1 frozen pie shell—   **garlic salt**
   unbaked   **dill weed**
½ c. margarine or butter   **3 eggs**
3-4 medium zucchini   **8 oz. Monterey Jack cheese**

Peel and slice zucchini. Saute in margarine or butter and generously sprinkle with garlic salt and dill weed. Saute about 8-10 minutes turning often. Drain on paper towels. Place zucchini in pie shell and cover evenly with sliced cheese. Beat eggs and pour over top of pie. Bake at 350° for 30-40 minutes. Serve hot.

"Delicious vegetable pie, not highly seasoned."

Rhea Abrams (Mrs. Samuel)
B. Abrams and Sons, Inc.
Harrisburg, Pennsylvania

"EASY KISHKE" or "MOCK DERMA"

Preparation Time: 15 minutes
Cooking Time: 1 hour, 15 minutes
Oven temperature: 350°

Serves: 12 pieces
Prepare ahead
Freeze

¼ lb. oleo
¾ c. hot water
1 c. flour
3 slices white bread,
  cubed

2 c. crushed corn flakes
½ c. chopped onions (fresh
  or frozen)
salt, pepper, garlic powder,
  paprika—to taste

Melt oleo in hot water. Add flour, bread, corn flakes and onions. Mix well. Add rest of ingredients. Use enough paprika to give reddish color. Have 2 pieces of aluminum foil ready, 15" long. Shape mixture into 2 long rolls; place on foil and roll and twist ends. Bake for 75 minutes at 350°. Cool; rewrap in fresh foil and freeze. When ready to use, place on cookie sheet and warm. Also can be heated with gravy.

"Can be used with meat or milk (parve) and inexpensive."

Millie Meyer (Mrs. Charles)
U. S. Scrap Iron & Metals, Inc.
Conneaut, Ohio

23

PISSALADIERE

Preparation Time: ½ hour to 45 minutes *Serves: 6*
Cooking Time: 15-20 minutes *Prepare Ahead*
Oven Temperature: 400°

Pie Crust
1¼ c. sifted flour
6 tbsp. sweet butter
3 tbsp. cold water
1 tsp. salt
2 tbsp. vegetable
  shortening

Filling
2 tsp. anchovy paste
dried sweet basil, to taste
3 large onions
olive oil
8 slices Emmenthal cheese
  (swigs)
Greek olives (pitted)
anchovies
1½ lbs. peeled cherry
  tomatoes or tomato
  wedges

Pie Crust Make a well in flour and salt mixed together. Add butter and shortening; cut in until mixture resembles coarse meal. Add water to form ball. Work on board with heel of hand a couple of times to distribute fat. Refrigerate a minimum of 1 hour to allow flour to rest. Line a pie plate (10" pyrex) with dough.

Filling Mince onions. Saute in olive oil until hot and translucent, but not brown. (Remove all moisture or pie will be soggy.) Brush bottom of pie crust with anchovy paste. Add basil. Add the onions and top with slices of cheese. Add the peeled tomatoes and put Greek olives wrapped in anchovies in between the tomatoes. Brush generously with olive oil and basil and bake at 400° for 15 to 20 minutes or until tomatoes look slightly brown. Let cool before serving.

"French pizza—a great alternative."

Sylvia Freedman (Mrs. Jake)
R. K. Freedman & Son Inc.
Green Island, New York

MUSHROOM BLINTZES

Preparation Time: ½-1 hour
Cooking Time: 20 minutes
Oven Temperature: 350°

Serves: 3 dozen
Prepare Ahead
Freeze

Filling
¼ c. parve margarine
1 onion, finely minced
1 lb. mushrooms, chopped
⅛ tsp. garlic powder
½ tsp. salt
⅛ tsp. freshly ground
    pepper
1 egg
¼ c. bread crumbs
1 tbsp. minced parsley

Batter
4 eggs, beaten
1⅓ c. water
½ tsp. salt
2 tbsp. oil
1 c. flour

Filling   Saute mushrooms and onions in margarine. Turning heat high after a few minutes so that mixture dries. Remove from heat. Mix remaining ingredients in thoroughly.

Batter   Mix ingredients listed above. Allow batter to set 1 hour in refrigerator before using. Heat 5″ frying pan which was greased lightly. Pour in small amount of batter. When batter starts to brown, turn out onto a towel to cool. Continue until all batter is used.

To Fill   Place 1 tbsp. filling on browned side, at one edge. Roll up, folding the sides in. Continue this procedure filling pieces. At this point blintzes may be refrigerated or frozen for future use.

To Serve   Either fry in a little hot margarine, until lightly browned on all sides, or place in shallow baking pan, brush with melted margarine and bake in 350° oven for 20 minutes or until lightly browned.

"These are delicious and different finger appetizers."

Celina G. Riebman (Mrs. Ronald)
Penn Del Salvage, Inc.
Wilmington, Delaware

CHEESE AND SPINACH ROULADE ROLL

Preparation Time: 45 to 50 minutes
Cooking Time: 55 minutes
Oven Temperature: 350°

Serves: 12
Prepare Ahead
  (make sauce
  same day)
Freeze

Roll
4 eggs, separated
¼ lb. butter
¾ c. flour
pinch of salt
1 c. milk
Parmesan cheese

Filling
2 10 oz. pkg. chopped
  spinach
¼ c. chopped onion
¼ c. grated cheddar
  cheese
2 tbsp. butter
½ tsp. salt
½ c. sour cream

Sauce
2 tbsp. butter
½ tsp. dry mustard
2 tbsp. flour
¼ tsp. salt
1 c. milk
1 c. grated cheddar cheese
dash pepper

Roll Melt butter. Stir in flour and salt with whisk. Slowly, add milk and cook until smooth. In another bowl, beat yolks; add small amount of milk mixture to yolk and beat lightly with fork. Add remaining mixture. Beat egg whites until stiff. Fold whites into milk mixture. Turn into jelly roll pan, lined with greased waxed paper. Bake in 350° oven for 12 to 15 minutes.

Filling Saute onion in butter. Thaw spinach and drain well. Add spinach, salt, cheddar cheese and sour cream to onion. Mix well.

Sauce Heat butter until melted and golden. Remove from heat. Add flour, salt, pepper and mustard. Stir. Add milk slowly, stirring constantly. Return to heat. Over medium heat, bring to boil, stirring constantly. Reduce heat and simmer 3 minutes.

Add cheese and stir until melted. *May add dry sherry to taste.

Assemble   Invert baked roll on waxed paper sprinkled with Parmesan cheese. Peel paper. Spread evenly with spinach. Roll starting with long side.

To Serve   Preheat oven to 350° and bake for 40 minutes. Slice and serve with sauce.

"Also excellent as a brunch entree."

Sherry Shulman (Mrs. Stephen)
I. Shulman & Son Co., Inc.
Elmira, New York

PRUNE BREAD

Preparation Time: ¼ hour
Cooking Time: 45 minutes
Oven Temperature: 350°

Servings: 8-10
Prepare Ahead
Freeze

1 pkg. of dried prunes
1 c. sugar
1 egg
2 tbsp. shortening
1 c. flour, white

1 c. flour, graham or wheat
2 tsp. baking powder
½ tsp. baking soda
pinch of salt

Cook prunes, cover with water and simmer until soft. Cut up ⅔ c. of prunes and fill to 1 c. with juice. Beat together, sugar, egg and 2 tbsp. shortening. In separate bowl, sift together flour, baking powder, baking soda and salt. Add to sugar mixture alternately with the cut up prunes and juice. Bake in bread pan at 350° for about 45 minutes or until top cracks.

"Coffee time treat."

Helen Dorangrichia
Miller Compressing Company
Milwaukee, Wisconsin

SPINACH & EGGPLANT CROUQUETTES

Preparation Time: 1 hour

Serves: About 50
Prepare Ahead

2 pkg. frozen chopped
  spinach
1 large eggplant (cubed
  with skin removed)
2 eggs
4 slices bacon (after
  cooking break into bits)
1 c. Parmesan cheese

1 clove garlic
1 small grated onion
salt
pepper
oregano
bread crumbs (about 2 cups)

Cook spinach according to package; drain well. Pan-broil bacon with garlic, remove bacon, discard garlic, and saute eggplant about 10 minutes with grated onion (pan covered). With potato masher, mash eggplant mixture. Mixture will be smooth with small lumps. Add to it the spinach, 1 beaten egg, bacon, cheese. Season with salt, pepper, oregano, and bread crumbs. If eggplant mixture is not stiff enough to form into shapes no larger than 1" x 1" x 2½" you may refrigerate it. Form into small shapes as desired, dip into beaten egg then roll in bread crumbs and fry in 2 tbsp. fat until golden (2-4 minutes). Drain on paper.

"Serve hot or cold with grey poupon mustard."

Joan Paske (Mrs. Matthew)
Luria Brothers, Inc.
Peoria, Illinois

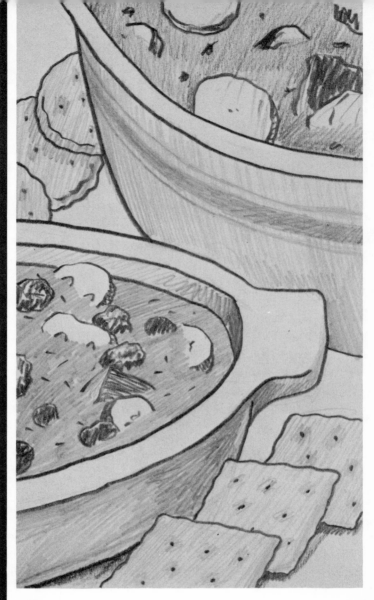

Soups

ROSA LEVIN'S PICKLE BORSHT

Preparation Time: 10 minutes plus 1 hour to ripen and 2 hours to chill

Serves: 4
Prepare Ahead

2 medium cucumbers
3 stalks fresh green dill
(to yield 25 lacey green
leaves producing 1 tsp.
chopped dill)
½ tsp. salt

4 tbsp. vinegar
1 medium garlic clove
(optional)
½ tbsp. sugar
sour cream

Peel and dice cucumbers into medium sized pieces. Wash dill thoroughly and cut leaves into very fine pieces. Mince clove of garlic into small pieces and add these ingredients to a quart jar filled with cold water. Add salt, vinegar, and sugar. Then stir well with spoon. Allow to ripen at room temperature for 1 hour. Then cover and refrigerate for 2 hours. When serving, add 1 heaping tbsp. sour cream per bowl, slowly blending borsht broth into bowl until milky. Spoon cucumber pieces and dill into bowl to rim.

"A piquant cold borsht, delicately blending cucumbers, dill and seasonings."

Saralee Levin (Mrs. Howard)
Myer Levin & Sons, Inc.
Warsaw, Indiana

CUCUMBER SOUP I

Preparation Time: 4 minutes

Serves: 3
Prepare Ahead

1 10¾ oz. can cream of
celery soup, undiluted
1 c. whole milk
1 c. cottage cheese
¼ c. coarsely chopped
cucumber

2 tbsp. coarsely chopped
green (bell) pepper
1 tsp. coarsely chopped
onion
caviar

Combine all ingredients in container of electric blender except caviar. Process until smooth. Chill. Serve with 1 tsp. caviar on top.

"A light soup, summer or winter."

John B. Fisher
Biltmore Iron & Metal Co., Inc.
Asheville, North Carolina

CUCUMBER SOUP II

Preparation Time: 45 minutes *Serves: 6*
Cooking Time: 20 to 25 minutes *Prepare Ahead*

2 large cucumbers
2 tbsp. butter
6 tbsp. shallots or onions
4 to 4½ c. chicken stock
  or chicken broth

4 to 5 tbsp. cream of wheat
1 tsp. red wine vinegar
½ c. sour cream
1 tsp. dill weed

Peel cucumbers and cut in half lengthwise. Scoop out seeds and slice. Chop shallots or onions and saute in butter. Add chicken stock or broth, cucumbers, vinegar and dill weed. Bring to a boil and stir in cream of wheat. Cover and simmer for 20 to 25 minutes. Puree in food processor or blender. Add sour cream; reheat and serve.

"Delicious, creamy soup with a surprising taste."

JoAnne Witherspoon (Mrs. David)
David Witherspoon, Inc.
Knoxville, Tennessee

GAZPACHO I

Preparation Time: 30 to 45 minutes

Serves: 12 to 15
Prepare Ahead
Freeze

1 lg. can tomato juice
2 lg. cucumbers, diced
2 lg. firm tomatoes, diced
1 lg. green pepper, diced
2 tsp. parsley, chopped
½ pkg. onion soup mix
2 tbsp. olive oil
2 tbsp. Worcestershire
  sauce

½ c. wine vinegar
¼ c. white vinegar
½ c. sherry
3 dashes Tabasco sauce
½ tsp. Accent
½ tsp. garlic powder
½ tsp. celery salt
½ tsp. salt
10 turns ground pepper

Mix all ingredients together. Run half of completed recipe through blender. Mix together and chill for 4 hours. Serve in large, hollowed green pepper, anchored in a dish of crushed ice and top with thin slice of unpeeled cucumber.

"Cold, spicy, delicious. Great for summertime."

Polly Winfield (Mrs. David)
Versatile Metals
Bensenville, Illinois

GAZPACHO II

Preparation Time: ½ hour

Serves: 6
Prepare Ahead
Freeze

6 ripe tomatoes, peeled &
  chopped (3 cups)
1 medium cucumber,
  peeled, seeded &
  chopped (1 cup)
1 small onion, finely
  chopped (½ cup)
1 small green pepper,
  finely chopped (½ cup)

1 small clove garlic, minced
1½ c. tomato juice
¼ c. olive oil
2 tbsp. vinegar
1 tsp. salt
⅛ tsp. pepper
few drops of bottled hot
  pepper sauce

In a large mixing bowl combine the chopped tomato, cucumber, onion, green pepper, garlic, tomato juice, olive oil, vinegar, salt, pepper and pepper sauce. Chill until serving time. Serve in bowls or individual icers. Top with toasted bread cubes or croutons.

"A perky change of pace from the usual soups!"

Lauri Samuels
Sinaiko Bros.
Division of H. Samuels Co.
Portage, Wisconsin

GAZPACHO SOUP III

Preparation Time: 20-30 minutes   *Serves: 4-6*
Prepare Ahead

1 can 10½ oz. tomato soup
1 can water (10½ oz.)
2 tbsp. olive oil
2 tbsp. wine vinegar
1 small cucumber,
   washed, seeded, sliced
½ c. green pepper
¼ c. onion, cut fine
1 small clove garlic, pressed
salt
pepper
red cayenne pepper to taste

Using the blender, mix thoroughly after adding each ingredient. This helps to keep soup from separating. Mix well; chill in refrigerator. Serve cold.

Additional small thin slices of refrigerated cucumber can be served in soup.

"Piquant—refreshing—simple—elegant, with a delightful tomato base."

Marilyn W. Griescdieck
(Mrs. Henry)
American Pulverizer
St. Louis, Missouri

33

DOTTIE'S TURKEY SOUP

Preparation and Cooking Time: 5-6
*   hours total*

Serves: 8-10
Freeze
Prepare Ahead

1 turkey carcass
water
2 bay leaves
salt & pepper
¼ tsp. each marjoram,
   thyme & basil
2 tbsp. butter
1 can consomme
3 tbsp. whole wheat flour
½ c. uncooked brown rice

¾ c. chopped celery
turkey meat
turkey gravy
turkey dressing
1 lb. chestnut puree
2 c. fresh mushrooms
   (sliced)
⅓ c. peanut oil
Madeira wine

Remove all meat from turkey carcass, break up carcass and put it into a large pot. Cover with water, put in the bay leaves, marjoram, thyme, basil, salt, and pepper. Let it simmer slowly for at least 4 hours. Remove the bones and strain the broth through a sieve. Melt 2 tbsp. butter in a large saucepan, stir into it the 3 tbsp. flour until smooth. Gradually stir in the stock, which should be about 2 qts. Bring it to a boil. Now add the rice, celery, additional salt and pepper to taste and cook gently until rice is soft (approx. 25-30 minutes). Saute 2 cups sliced fresh mushrooms in peanut oil and add them to the soup. Heat chestnut puree and dilute with a can of consomme. Add to the soup along with any leftover gravy and dressing you may have. Let all this simmer gently for about 25-30 minutes. Just before serving, stir in 3 tbsp. Madeira wine.

"It may seem like a lot of work, but it's worth it, wait until you taste it."

Dottie Holak
Miller Compressing Company
Milwaukee, Wisconsin

SOUP CONTINENTAL

Preparation Time: 10 minutes
Cooking Time: 15 to 20 minutes

Serves: 8 to 10
Prepare Ahead
Freeze

¼ c. butter or margarine
1 c. turkey or chicken,
  cooked and chopped
2 tbsp. onion, finely
  chopped
2 c. potatoes, diced,
  uncooked
1 c. celery, diced
2 c. turkey broth or
  chicken bouillon

1 #303 can cream-style corn
1⅔ c. evaporated milk
1 tsp. salt
¼ tsp. paprika
¼ tsp. pepper
¼ tsp. ginger
2 tbsp. parsley, chopped

Melt butter over low heat. Add turkey and onion; cook until onion is transparent. Add potatoes, celery and broth. Cook until potatoes and celery are tender, 10 to 15 minutes. Add corn, milk and seasonings. Heat thoroughly, but do not boil, stirring occasionally.

"An elegant soup made from ingredients usually on hand."

Marilyn Cassidy (Mrs. David)
Vulcan Materials Co.
Birmingham, Alabama

VEGETABLE SOUP NIVERNAIS

Preparation Time: 15 minutes
Cooking Time: 60 minutes

Serves: 8 to 10
Prepare Ahead

¼ lb. plus 2 tbsp. butter
1 c. each carrots, turnips,
  leeks, celery and
  potatoes
1 tsp. salt
4 c. water
1 c. heavy cream

extra vegetables: 1 carrot
  1 small turnip
  1 stalk celery
salt—to taste
freshly ground white
  pepper—to taste

Melt ¼ lb. butter in deep, heavy kettle. Slice vegetables and add to melted butter and saute. Cover kettle tightly and stew over low heat 20 minutes. Add water and salt and bring to boil. Simmer 20 minutes. Strain, reserving liquid. Chop strained vegetables and return to liquid. Finely chop extra vegetables and saute in 2 tbsp. butter. Add to soup. Add cream, and correct seasonings. Serve hot or cold.

"Marvelous soup for vegetarians."

Susan Lipsett (Mrs. Shelly)
Lipsett Industries Corp.
New York, New York

BLACK BEAN SOUP

Preparation Time: 15 minutes
Cooking Time: 5½ hours

Serves: 6-8
Prepare Ahead
Freeze

1 small onion, sliced
2 stalks celery, chopped
1 ham bone or bits of
  leftover ham
2 tsp. salt
2 tsp. pepper

1 tsp. dry mustard
few grains cayenne (or
  Tabasco sauce)
2 c. dried black beans (12
  oz. pkg.)
2 qt. cold water

Combine black beans and water in large kettle. Bring to boiling point and simmer 10 minutes. Cover and set aside 1 hour. Then add remaining ingredients. Cover and simmer 3 to 4 hours until beans are soft. (In crockpot simmer on low for about 12 hours.) Add water if needed to make about 1½ qts. Serve with additional chopped onions.

"Like regular bean soup only darker in color and hotter tasting."

Tiffany Francis (Mrs. Terry)
Adirondack Steel Specialties
Albany, New York

CLAM CHOWDER

Preparation Time: 30 minutes
Cooking Time: 1-2 hours

Serves: 10
Prepare Ahead
Freeze

⅓ c. celery, sliced
⅓ c. onion, sliced
¼ c. green pepper, sliced
2½ c. clams, drained, reserve juice
2½ c. clam juice
½ c. potato, sliced
salt & pepper to taste

dash Worcestershire sauce
dash Tabasco
dash thyme
¾ c. flour
1 c. melted butter
2 c. half & half
1¾ c. milk

Saute celery, onion and green pepper in small amount of butter. Add clam juice and juice from clams and bring to a boil. Add potatoes; simmer until potatoes are done. Mix flour and butter to make roux; add to vegetables. Stir constantly until smooth and thick. Heat milk and half and half; add to vegetable mixture. Stir in clams, salt, pepper, Worcestershire, Tabasco and thyme. Simmer 1-2 hours or longer to bring out flavors.

"Easy to prepare—tastes better each time it is reheated."

Linda Minter (Mrs. Michael)
Scrap Metal Processors, Inc.
Minneapolis, Minnesota

37

ONION SOUP

Preparation Time: 90 minutes   *Serves: 7 to 8*
Cooking Time: 50 minutes

6 to 7 c. thinly sliced yellow onion	**3 tbsp. butter**
½ c. olive oil	**3 oz. grated Parmesan cheese**
1¼ tsp. salt	**3 oz. grated baby Swiss cheese**
⅛ tsp. pepper	**cognac**
3 tbsp. flour	**7 c. good beef stock**
1½ bay leaves	**1 small onion, grated**
1¼ tsp. sage	**French bread**
1¼ c. good red wine	
⅛ tsp. thyme	

Slice onions. Melt 2 tbsp. butter and 2 tbsp. olive oil in pan. Add onions and stir until coated over moderate heat. Cover and cook until tender, about 15 to 20 minutes. Stir once or twice. Remove cover; add salt and pepper and brown onions for 5 minutes. Sprinkle flour over onions and add 1 tbsp. butter. Brown flour for 5 minutes. Mixture will become pasty. Add beef stock, wine and seasonings and simmer for ½ hour. Slice French bread 1" thick and coat slices with balance of olive oil with pastry brush. Bake in oven at 300° for 20 to 30 minutes. Put hot soup in bowls. Add 1 tsp. of cognac. Float 1 piece of the French bread on top. Add small amount of grated raw onion. Then alternate layers of Swiss cheese and Parmesan cheese. Place under broiler to melt and brown cheese being careful not to burn. Serve hot.

"Classic French Onion Soup."

William V. C. Webster
Pittsburgh Alloys Inc.
West Mifflin, Pennsylvania

MUSHROOM-BARLEY SOUP

Preparation Time: 1 hour
Cooking Time: 2½ to 3 hours

Serves: 40 (use
soup mugs)
Prepare ahead
Freeze

**1 turkey carcass and
  bones**
Water to cover (8 quarts)
**4 large onions, cut in
  quarters**
**1 bunch celery, cut in
  small pieces**
**6 large carrots, cut in
  small pieces**
**18 to 20 beef bouillon
  cubes—to taste**

1 box barley (16 oz.)
2 bay leaves
**2 lbs. fresh mushrooms,
  chopped in *small pieces*
  or run through food
  processor (be sure *not* to
  puree)**
**½ tsp. ground fresh black
  pepper (or to taste)**
salt—to taste

Bring first 5 ingredients to a boil in large soup pot. Skim top. Add bouillon cubes and simmer 1 hour. Remove carcass and bones. Discard. Strain vegetables, reserving liquid. Put vegetables in food processors or blender and puree. Add vegetables, barley, bay leaves, mushrooms and pepper to liquid. Simmer very slowly, stirring frequently until barley is done. (About 1 to 1½ hours.) Be careful barley doesn't stick to pot and burn.

"A great way to use those Thanksgiving turkey bones."

Mary Jean Cohen (Mrs. Wilbur)
Cohen Brothers, Inc.
Middletown, Ohio

MUSHROOM SOUP WITH PARMESAN CHEESE

Preparation Time: 10 minutes
Cooking Time: 20-30 minutes

Serves: 4
Prepare Ahead

1 tbsp. butter
1 tbsp. olive oil
1 medium onion, grated
1 clove garlic, split
1 lb. mushroom caps,
   sliced thin
3 tbsp. tomato paste
3 c. chicken stock
2 tbsp. sweet Italian
   Vermouth

½ tsp. salt
dash pepper
Garniture: 4 egg yolks
   2 tbsp. parsley, finely
     chopped
   2½ tbsp. Parmesan
     cheese, grated
   4 slices Italian bread

Soup   In a heavy pan melt butter and olive oil. Saute onion and garlic, letting them brown gently. Discard garlic. Stir in mushrooms and saute for 5 minutes. Add tomato paste and mix well. Add chicken stock and stir. Add Italian Vermouth. Add salt and pepper to taste. Let simmer 10 minutes.

Garniture   Beat together egg yolks, parsley and Parmesan cheese. Cut about 1 inch thick slices Italian bread. Place one slice in each bowl. Beat egg mixture into boiling soup and serve at once poured over the bread slices.

"Fabulously different mushroom soup for a cold, drizzly night."

> Karen B. Strelitz
> Metal Briquetting Company
> Long Beach, California

MEXICAN DELITE

Preparation Time: 60 minutes   *Serves: 4 to 8*
Cooking Time: 40 minutes   *Prepare Ahead*

**3 tbsp. butter (butter
  substitute, oleo or
  chicken bouillon)**
2 tbsp. dried onion
**1 28 oz. can peeled
  tomatoes, cut into
  pieces (reserve liquid)**
**1 4 oz. can diced green
  chilies**

1 2 oz. jar pimentos, diced
**1 lb. cheddar cheese, diced
  or grated**
salt & pepper, to taste
**Optional: Mushrooms and/or
  green beans**

Combine butter (butter substitute, oleo or chicken bouillon)
and onion in soup pot. Cover and cook on high heat, stirring
a few times. (In microwave, cook on high for 7 minutes.) Add
tomatoes and liquid, chilies, pimentos, salt and pepper and
blend well. Cover and cook on high heat until mixture comes
to full boil. (In microwave about 9 to 10 minutes.) Stir in cheese
and salt and pepper to taste.* Continue cooking on high heat
until cheese is almost melted. (In microwave about 1 minute.)
Serve hot.

*If using mushrooms and/or green beans, add at same time as
cheese.

If additional bulk is desired, serve over bed of heated bean
sprouts.

"This recipe is great for dieters and non-dieters alike; extremely tasty and filling."

**Annette Federow (Mrs. Harry)
Federow Iron & Metal Co.
Springfield, Missouri**

A PRACTICAL GUIDE TO EQUIVALENTS

Apples . . . . 3 pounds = 2 quarts, sliced

Butter . . . . 1 stick = ½ cup
                                            4 sticks = 1 pound
                                            1 pound = 2½ cups

Cheese
  Cottage . . . . ½ pound = 1 cup
  Cream . . . . 3 ounces = 6 tablespoons
  Cheddar . . . . ¼ pound = 1 cup, shredded
  Parmesan . . . . ¼ pound = 1 cup, grated

Chocolate . . . . 1 ounce = 3 to 4 tablespoons, grated

Cornstarch . . . . 1 tablespoon = 2 tablespoons flour

Eggs
  Whole . . . . 1 egg = 3 tablespoons = 2 ounces
                                            5 to 6 eggs = 1 cup
  Whites . . . . 1 white = 2 tablespoons
                                            8 to 10 whites = 1 cup
  Yolks . . . . 1 yolk = 1 tablespoon
                                            14 to 16 yolks = 1 cup

Flour (It is best to weigh flour)
  Unsifted . . . . 1 pound = 3 cups
  All-purpose, sifted once . . . 1 pound = 3¾ cups
  Cake, sifted once . . . . 1 pound = 2 cups

Gelatin . . . . 1 envelope (Knox) = 1 tablespoon

Graham Crackers . . . . 3 cups crumbs = 30 to 36 crackers

Continued on page 50

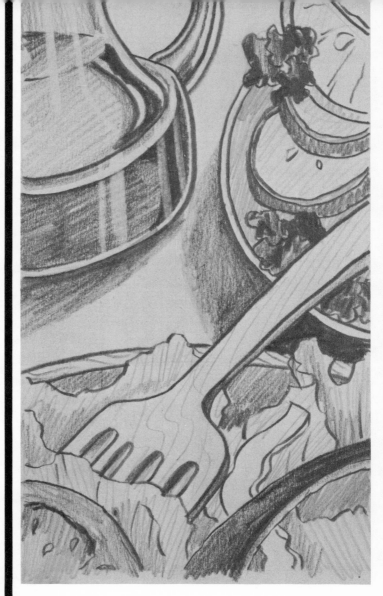

Salads

CAULIFLOWER SALAD

Preparation Time: 30 minutes   *Serves: 12*
                                        Prepare Ahead

1 head iceberg lettuce   **¼ c. Parmesan cheese**
1 head cauliflower, sliced   **2 c. Hellmann's mayonnaise**
** thin**   **2 tbsp. sugar**
1 small onion, chopped
1 lb. bacon, cooked and
** crumbled**

Layer first 5 ingredients listed above in 6 qt. bowl in order given. Spread 2 c. mayonnaise over the top. Seal the top leaving no holes or cracks. Sprinkle 2 tbsp. sugar over mayonnaise. Cover with Saran Wrap and let stand overnight in refrigerator. Toss and serve.

"A refreshing tossed cauliflower and lettuce salad."

Pixie Carrier (Mrs. Greg)
Scrap Corporation of America
Chicago, Illinois

SNOW PEA SALAD

Preparation Time: 15 minutes   *Serves: 6*
                                        Prepare Ahead
                                        (add dressing
                                        later)

Salad   **Dressing**
1 lb. snow peas   **juice of ½ lemon**
3 to 4 scallions, slivered   **¼ tsp. dry mustard**
Bibb or leaf lettuce   **1 tsp. anchovy paste**
                                    1 tsp. honey
                                    dash Tabasco
                                    5 to 6 tbsp. olive oil
                                    salt and pepper to taste

Salad   Remove strings from snow peas. Cook in rapidly boiling water 1 to 2 minutes; refresh under cold running water. Drain and dry. Line bowl with pieces of bibb or leaf lettuce. Add snow peas and slivered scallions. Toss with enough dressing to cover.

Dressing   Mix together all ingredients and chill.

"Light and crisp salad. Easy to make."

> **Lois Lefton (Mrs. Benjamin)**
> **Lefton Iron & Metal**
> **East St. Louis, Illinois**

FROZEN GREEN PEA SALAD

Preparation Time: 20 minutes   *Serves: 6*
                                        Prepare Ahead

1 head lettuce   **1 c. mayonnaise**
4 stalks celery   **⅓ c. milk**
4 small green onion stalks   **½ c. crumbled bacon**
1 10 oz. pkg. frozen green
  peas

Chop lettuce and place in bottom of 8" glass baking dish to make thick layer. Chop celery and green onions and place on top of lettuce. Pour frozen peas on top. Mix together mayonnaise and milk and whip with fork until smooth. (Don't make too thin.) Spread milk mixture thickly on top of peas. Thickly spread crumbled bacon on top of milk mixture. Keep in refrigerator at least 4 hours before serving. Salad is better if made the day before serving.

"Cool and refreshing compliment to any meal."

> **Mrs. Ted Ward**
> **N. C. Hide & Fur Co.**
> **Rocky Mount, North Carolina**

COLD RICE SALAD I

Preparation Time: 30 minutes
Cooking Time: 20 minutes

Serves: 6 to 8
Prepare Ahead
Freeze

1 pkg. chicken flavored
rice (Rice-a-Roni or any
brand)
1 small green pepper,
chopped
3 green onions, chopped

1 jar marinated artichoke
hearts, chopped (save
juice)
1 small can chopped black
olives
⅓ c. mayonnaise

Cook rice to package directions. Chop all other ingredients. When rice is done, mix with all chopped ingredients. (Drain artichokes and save the juice.) In small bowl, mix mayonnaise and juice of artichokes together. Pour over rice mixture, and stir in. Chill well before serving.

"This is a wonderfully easy recipe, which your company will think you went to lots of trouble to prepare."

Linda Segal (Mrs. Steven)
J. L. Proler Iron & Steel Co.
Houston, Texas

COLD RICE SALAD II

Preparation Time: 30 minutes
Cooking Time: 18 minutes

Serves: 12
Prepare Ahead

3 c. water
1½ tsp. salt
1½ c. long grain rice
2 tbsp. dry white wine
2 green peppers, finely
diced
½ c. diced cucumbers,
seeds removed

½ c. canned peas
¼ c. wine vinegar
¼ c. olive oil
1 tsp. oregano
2 shallots, minced
salt & pepper—to taste

In a large saucepan, bring rice to boil in salted water. (Add rice gradually so water does not stop boiling, when rice is added.) Cook for about 18 minutes, uncovered. Stir in wine. Transfer rice to a bowl and let cool. Combine green peppers, cucumbers and peas in another bowl and add to rice mixture. Combine well. Combine wine vinegar, oil, oregano, shallots, salt and pepper. Pour this dressing over the rice salad and toss it well. Spoon the salad into a serving dish lined with lettuce leaves and refrigerate until cold. May be served as a salad or as a vegetable.

"This is a refreshing cold, crunchy salad."

> **Rosann Peck (Mrs. B. David)**
> **Peck Iron & Metal Co., Inc.**
> **Richmond, Virginia**

CHINESE SPINACH SALAD

Preparation Time: 20 minutes　　　　　*Serves: 5 to 6*

Dressing
½ c. safflower oil
¼ c. soy sauce
2 tbsp. fresh lemon juice
1½ tbsp. grated onion
1½ tbsp. sesame seeds
½ tsp. sugar
½ tsp. pepper

Salad
1 bag fresh spinach
½ lb. sliced mushrooms
1 small container sliced
　water chestnuts
fresh or canned beansprouts
¼ c. seasoned croutons

Mix dressing ingredients. Marinate mushrooms and water chestnuts for 24 hours. Serve dressing over spinach and fresh or canned beansprouts. Dress salad 10 minutes before serving. Put croutons on top.

"You may want to double this recipe because there will be requests for more!"

> **Rena Haveson (Mrs. Paul)**
> **Charles Bluestone Company**
> **Elizabeth, Pennsylvania**

47

EAST INDIAN TUNA SALAD

Preparation Time: 45 minutes   *Serves: 6*
Cooking Time: 20 minutes for buttered   *Prepare Ahead*
  toast or rye krisp
Oven Temperature: 200°

2 6½ oz. cans of tuna
1 c. celery, chopped
⅓ c. stuffed olives, sliced
⅓ c. ripe olives, chopped
⅓ c. sweet pickles,
  chopped
⅓ c. pimento, chopped
  (optional)

½ c. almonds, slivered
buttered white bread or rye
  krisp or buttered toast
⅔ c. mayonnaise
1 tbsp. lemon juice
2 tsp. curry powder
3-6 cantaloupes—depending
  on size

Run hot water over cans of opened tuna fish. Drain and cool. Add chopped celery, olives, sweet pickles and almonds. Mix mayonnaise, lemon juice and curry powder. Add this mixture to tuna mixture and blend well. To serve place center cut slices of cantaloupe, about ½"-¾" thick, on plate and fill cantaloupe ring with ⅓-½ cup of tuna filling. Garnish with 4-6 cantaloupe balls or mandarin orange slices and pineapple cubes. Decorate with mint tips or watercress. Serve with buttered toast, crackers, or rolls.

"Pleasing to the eye and an unusual combination of cantaloupe and tuna."

Dorothy S. Nudelman
S. J. Nudelman and Son, Inc.
Portland, Oregon

VINEGARETTE DRESSING

Preparation Time: 20 minutes
Makes: ½ gallon

Prepare Ahead
Freeze

2 c. sugar
2 c. vinegar
1 tsp. white pepper
1 tsp. dry mustard
1 tsp. salt

1 tsp. paprika
juice of small onion, grated
3½ c. Wesson oil
1 egg yolk (extra large, well
  beaten)

Combine dry ingredients and mix well. Add vinegar and oil alternately; mix using electric beaters. Add well beaten egg yolk.

"This is a very tasty vinegarette dressing."

Terry Blumberg (Mrs. Robert)
The Loef Co., Inc.
Athens, Georgia

Honey . . . . 1 pound = 1¼ cups
Lemon . . . . 1 average = 2 to 3 tablespoons
                               juice
Macaroni . . . . 1 cup dry (4 ounces) = 2¼
                               cups cooked
Maple Syrup . . . . 12 ounces = 1½ cups
Noodles . . . . 1½ cups dry (4 ounces) = 2¼
                               cups cooked
Nuts . . . . 1 cup chopped = ¼ pound
Onions . . . . 1 medium = ½ cup chopped
Potatoes (white) . . . . 1 pound raw, unpared = 2 cups
                               mashed
Raisins (seedless) . . . . 1 pound = 3 cups
Rice . . . . 1 cup dry = 3 to 3½ cups
                               cooked
Sugar
  Brown . . . . 1 pound = 2½ cups
  Confectioners' (sifted) . . . . . 1 pound = 3½ cups
  Granulated . . . . 1 pound = 2 cups
Tomatoes . . . . 1 pound = 3 medium

Entrees

FRIED CHICKEN WITH CASHEWS

Preparation Time: 20 to 30 minutes
Cooking Time: 15 minutes

Serves: 4
Prepare Ahead
(stir-frying
should be done
just before
serving)

Chicken
2-3 chicken breasts
   (approx. 1 lb.)
1 c. whole cashews
2 dried red peppers,
   soaked 20 minutes,
   chopped
1 leek, cut in ½ inch
   pieces
½ inch piece fresh ginger,
   peeled and chopped
2 green peppers, cut in ½
   inch cubes
4-5 c. vegetable oil

A-Sauce
1 egg
¼ tsp. salt
1 tbsp. cooking sherry or
   cocktail sherry (dry)
¼ tsp. msg (opt.)
½ tsp. baking powder
5 dashes pepper
1½ tbsp. cornstarch
1 tbsp. vegetable oil

B-Sauce
2 tbsp. soy sauce
1 tbsp. vinegar
1 tbsp. sugar
1 tbsp. sherry
½ tsp. msg (opt.)
2 tsp. cornstarch
4 tsp. water
2 tbsp. chicken broth

A-Sauce Combine all ingredients and mix until smooth.
B-Sauce Mix cornstarch and water together until smooth. Add to remaining ingredients and mix.
Chicken Bone chicken and cut into ½ inch cubes and marinate in A-Sauce for 10 to 15 minutes. Meanwhile heat 4 c. of vegetable oil in a wok (oil should reach half-way up the wok) untiil very hot, but not smoking. (Test oil by dropping a little

marinade in and if it immediately comes to the top of the oil, it is hot enough.) When hot, place all chicken and marinade in oil and separate with chop sticks. Fry until chicken turns white (4 to 5 minutes), then add cashews and fry 2 more minutes. Place green peppers (which have been cut up) on a strainer or metal collander and pour chicken, cashews and oil over green peppers draining oil into another container (this cooks the peppers just slightly so they are still crisp). In empty wok or frypan put 2 tbsp. vegetable oil and when hot stir fry leek, ginger, and red pepper for 1 to 2 minutes. Add chicken, cashews and green peppers and fry, mixing gently with a wooden spoon for 1 to 2 minutes. Add B-Sauce and heat until warm and thick. Serve with rice.

"A tangy Chinese Chicken dish with crisp vegetables and nuts."

Marsha and Jerry Rosenberg
Lake City, Inc.
Cleveland, Ohio

CHICKEN CACCIATORE

Serves: 4

1 fryer cut-up (or 4
  chicken breasts—8
  pieces)
¼ c. oil
2 medium onions, sliced
2 cloves garlic, minced
2 cans tomato sauce

1 tsp. oregano
¼ tsp. tabasco sauce
1 green pepper, cleaned and
  sliced
¼ c. red wine
½ c. water

In skillet, brown chicken parts in oil. Remove chicken from pan. Add onions and garlic to pan; cook on low heat for 5 minutes. Stir in all other ingredients; add chicken pieces; cover and simmer for 30 minutes or until tender. Uncover and cook until sauce thickens a little.

Bernard Landau
M.S. Kaplan Company
Chicago, Illinois

COMPANY CHICKEN

Preparation Time: 1 hour   *Serves: 6*
Cooking Time: 1 hour
Oven Temperature: 350°

1-2 chickens, cut up (or selected pieces)
1 c. flour
1½ tsp. salt
pepper
2 tsp. paprika
2 c. celery, chopped to bite size pieces

1 can condensed cream of chicken soup
½ c. milk
2 tbsp. pimento, diced
1 c. American cheese, finely diced
2 c. soft bread cubes
½ c. almonds, slivered

Coat chicken with mixture of flour, salt, pepper, paprika. Lightly brown chicken in fat. Put celery in bottom of greased pan (covered roaster). Place chicken on top of celery. Combine soup, milk, pimento, cheese and pour over chicken. Cover with buttered bread crumbs. Sprinkle on almonds. Bake in moderate oven 350°, 1 hour, or until chicken tests done.

"All you need for a meal is a vegetable and salad and of course your usual drink and dessert if desired."

Rachel Blalock
Platnick Bros.
Bluefield, W. Virginia

PEPPER DUCK

Preparation Time: 15 minutes   *Serves: 2*
Cooking Time: 3 hours
Oven Temperature: 325°

1 duck per two persons
1 tbsp. freshly ground pepper

salt
choice of orange, apple or celery stalk for flavor

Stuff the duck with pieces of orange, apple or celery stalk. Cover oven-ready duck with heavy coat of coarse freshly ground pepper. The pepper will become less pungent and more "nutty" during cooking. Add salt. Roast on a rack in roasting pan at 325° for 3 hours, pricking skin frequently. It will be very crisp and fat free.

"Crisp, nutty flavored duck."

Shirley Richman (Mrs. John W.)
I. Richman Co., Inc.
Washington, Pennsylvania

CHICKEN CASSEROLE

Preparation Time: 1 hour
Cooking Time: 1 hour
Oven Temperature: 350°

Serves: 8
Prepare Ahead
Freeze

2 cans cut string beans
2 whole chicken breasts
1 can cream of celery
  soup
1 can cream of chicken
  soup
½ pt. sour cream

1 pkg. onion soup (dry)
1 pkg. Pepperidge Farm
  Stuffing
¾ c. water
1 stick butter

Put string beans on bottom of 9 x 13 pan. Lay chicken (cut up) on top. Mix onion soup and cans of soup in sour cream. Pour over chicken. Fix stuffing as per instructions on package and put on top of casserole. Cover with foil. Bake at 350° for 1 hour. Remove foil during last 15 minutes.

"A quick meal with a tangy flavor."

Bernice Noeker (Mrs. Raymond)
Suisman & Blumenthal
Hartford, Connecticut

ENTREES

EAST INDIA CHICKEN & RICE

Preparation Time: 20 minutes　　　　*Serves: 4-6*
Cooking Time: 45 minutes　　　　　*Prepare Ahead*
　　　　　　　　　　　　　　　　　　Freeze

1 2½ to 3 lb. broiler or
　fryer, cut up
¼ c. flour
1 tbsp. curry powder
1½ tsp. salt
½ tsp. pepper

3 chicken bouillon cubes
3 c. boiling water
1 large onion, thinly sliced
1 c. raisins
⅔ c. regular rice (not quick
　cooking)

Clean and rinse chicken. Combine flour, salt, pepper, curry powder in paper or plastic bag, add chicken pieces and shake to coat. Place pieces in pan and sprinkle onion, raisins, rice over chicken. Dissolve bouillon cubes in boiling water & pour over chicken. Reduce heat so liquid only simmers gently. Cover, simmer 45 minutes or until all ingredients are tender.

"Chicken and rice with pungent curry flavor."

Esther Deutch (Mrs. Sidney)
I. Deutch & Sons
Cincinnati, Ohio

CHICKEN PARISIENNE

Preparation Time: 25 minutes　　　　*Serves: 4 to 6*
Cooking Time: 1¼ to 1½ hours　　　*Prepare Ahead*
Oven Temperature: 350°

4 large or 6 medium
　chicken breasts, halved,
　skinned and boned
1 can condensed cream of
　mushroom soup

1 to 3 oz. can sliced
　mushrooms
1 c. dairy sour cream
½ c. cooking sherry
Paprika—to taste

Place chicken breasts in 9″ x 13″ baking dish. Combine remaining ingredients (including mushroom liquid); pour over chicken. Sprinkle generously with paprika. Bake in 350° oven 1¼ to 1½ hours or until tender. Serve with hot, fluffy rice.

"A festive, tasty dish with a minimum of preparation."

Dorothy Simon (Mrs. S. Howard)
Price-Watson Co.—Division of
General Iron Industries
Chicago, Illinois

ORANGE CHICKEN

Preparation Time: 10-15 minutes
Cooking Time: 45 minutes
Oven Temperature: 350°

Serves: 6
Prepare Ahead
Freeze

1 small can frozen orange
   juice, thawed
1½ cans water
2 tbsp. brown sugar

½ tsp. oregano
½ tsp. nutmeg
1 tbsp. cornstarch
6 chicken breasts, boned

Season chicken with salt and pepper and bake in 350° oven until almost done (about 25 minutes). Mix other ingredients and pour over chicken. Baste occasionally until sauce is thickened and chicken is done. Recipe can be doubled or tripled for an elegant company dinner and served with rice. Preserved kum-quats and parsley make a pretty garnish.

"This is a chicken with a piquant orange flavor, a pure party pleaser and low in calories."

Shirley Lans (Mrs. William)
William Lans Sons Co.
South Beloit, Illinois

COQ AU VIN

Preparation Time: 15 minutes
Cooking Time: 1½ hours
Oven Temperature: 400°

Serves: 4
Prepare Ahead

2 quartered broilers (2 pounders)
6 slices pastrami, diced
2 tbsp. parve margarine
8 whole mushrooms
8 small peeled white onions
⅔ c. sliced green onion
1 clove garlic, crushed
2½ tbsp. flour

1 tsp. salt
¼ tsp. dried thyme leaves
⅛ tsp. pepper
2 c. Burgundy
1 c. canned condensed chicken broth
8 small new scrubbed potatoes
chopped parsley

Wash chicken and dry on paper towels. Saute pastrami until crisp in Dutch oven; remove. Add margarine to drippings; heat. Add chicken and brown well. Remove. Pour off all but two tbsp. fat from Dutch oven. Add mushrooms and white onions to pot; cook until browned. Remove. Set aside with chicken. Add green onions and garlic to pot and saute two minutes. Remove from heat. Stir in flour, salt, thyme and pepper. Return to heat and cook, stirring constantly, until the flour is browned, approximately three minutes. Gradually stir in wine and chicken broth; bring to boil, stirring. Remove from heat. Stir in pastrami, chicken, onions and mushrooms. Refrigerate covered overnight. Next day, preheat oven to 400°. Add the potatoes to chicken mixture. Bake covered one and a half hours or until chicken and potatoes are tender.

"Superb version—delicious."

Jean R. Staiman (Mrs. Marvin)
Staiman Brothers
Williamsport, Pennsylvania

LEMON CHICKEN MARSALA

Preparation Time: 30 minutes　　*Serves: 4 to 6*
Cooking Time: 20 minutes　　*Prepare Ahead*

**4 boned & skinned
chicken breasts**
6 cloves of garlic
2 lemons
⅓ c. sweet marsala
**1 can Campbell's Chicken
Broth**
1 tsp. oregano
1 tsp. basil

**2 tbsp. fresh chopped
parsley**
3 tbsp. Wesson oil
3 tbsp. butter
**salt and fresh pepper, to
taste**
flour
**1 lb. fresh mushrooms,
sliced**

Cut each chicken breast into 6 strips. Coat with flour. Melt butter and oil in large skillet. Saute chicken quickly on both sides and remove. Press garlic into pan and saute quickly. Add mushrooms. If necessary, add more butter. When wilted add marsala and cook down for about 2 minutes. Add chicken broth slowly and juice of 1 lemon. If you wish a thicker sauce, add 1 tbsp. cornstarch mixed with a little water. Add basil, oregano, pepper and taste. If necessary, add salt. Cook for 5 minutes. Return chicken to sauce and the other lemon sliced in about 8 rounds on top of chicken. Sprinkle with parsley and cook on low heat for about 10 minutes.

This can be made in the morning, turned off, then reheated for dinner. Serve with green noodles and tossed salad.

"Breast of chicken with lemon, mushrooms and marsala sauce."

**Susan Gelman (Mrs. Warren)
Diversified Metals Corp.
St. Louis, Missouri**

BAKED CHICKEN CASSEROLE

Preparation Time: 30 minutes   *Serves: 10 to 12*
Cooking Time: 25 to 30 minutes   *Prepare Ahead*
Oven Temperature: 400°   *Freeze*

4 c. diced cooked chicken   **1 tsp. salt**
¾ c. mayonnaise   **2 tbsp. lemon juice**
1 can (10¾ oz.) cream of   **1 c. crushed potato chips**
**   chicken soup**   **   (Pringles work best)**
2 c. chopped celery   **⅔ c. grated cheddar cheese**
1 small onion, chopped   **⅓ c. chopped almonds**
4 hard boiled eggs,
**   chopped fine**

Saute celery and onion slightly. Mix first 8 ingredients. Put in oblong (13″ x 9″) baking pan. Combine crushed potato chips, cheddar cheese and almonds; sprinkle on top. Chill several hours or overnight. Bake at 400° for 25 to 30 minutes or until heated through.

"This is tasty and easy to make, great for guests."

Juanita Roark (Mrs. Carl)
Metal Exchange
St. Louis, Missouri

CHICKEN ORIENTAL

Preparation Time: 15 minutes after   *Serves: 8*
*   chicken is cooked*   *Prepare Ahead*
Cooking Time: 1 hour   *Freeze*
Oven Temperature: 350°

4 c. chicken, cut up   **¼ c. lemon juice**
2 c. celery, chopped   **1 tsp. salt**
1 small jar pimiento   **½ tsp. minced onion**
1 c. slivered almonds   **1 c. grated cheddar cheese**
½ c. mayonnaise   **1 can Chinese Noodles (for**
1 can undiluted cream of   **   topping)**
**   celery soup**

Mix all ingredients together and place in a baking pan. Top with Chinese Noodles. Bake 1 hour at 350°. Let set 15 minutes before serving.

"A delicious, attractive dish especially for buffets, or light supper."

Janet Weltmann (Mrs. Norman)
Marley's
Syracuse, New York

FANTASTIC CHICKEN CASSEROLE

Preparation Time: 1-1½ hours
Cooking Time: 40 minutes
Oven Temperature: 350°

Serves: 10-12
Prepare Ahead
Freeze (before it is cooked)

3 c. boiled chicken, chopped
4 eggs, boiled
2 c. cooked rice in chicken broth
1½ c. celery, chopped
1 c. mayonnaise
2 cans cream of mushroom soup

1 onion, chopped
1 tsp. salt
2 tbsp. lemon juice or 1 tbsp. real lemon
2 tbsp. oleo
2 c. bread crumbs
3 oz. slivered almonds

Grease casserole pan with butter; mix all ingredients except eggs, bread crumbs and almonds in a large mixing bowl. Pour ½ of mixture into dish. Slice eggs and add remaining mixture. Top with bread crumbs made from 6 or 7 Brown & Serve rolls that have been buttered and cooked. Sprinkle with slivered almonds. Refrigerate overnight. Bake uncovered in 350° oven for 40 minutes. Serve hot.

"A delicious casserole with a crunchy taste."

Carol C. Ellis (Mrs. James)
Ellis Metals' Inc.
Brundidge, Alabama

WRAPPED CHICKEN BREASTS SUPREME

Preparation Time: 1½ hours
Cooking Time: 1 hour
Oven Temperature: 350°

Serves: 4
Prepare Ahead
Freeze

4 chicken breasts—boned, halved and pounded flat
1¼ c. dry white wine
½ c. olive oil
3 cloves garlic, crushed
bay leaves, oregano, salt & pepper to taste
2 tbsp. grated Romano cheese

½ lb. crumbled feta cheese
½ lb. small curd creamy cottage cheese
½ lb. sliced mushrooms (fresh)
2 eggs
¼ c. chopped green onions
1 lb. phyllo leaves
1 lb. butter, melted

Marinate breasts in 1 c. white wine, olive oil, garlic, bay leaves, salt and pepper. Cover and refrigerate overnight. Next day, mix feta, cottage cheese, egg and salt and pepper to taste. In ¼ c. white wine, cook green onions and mushrooms until tender. Allow to cool and combine with grated Romano; then add to feta mixture.

Place marinated breast on flat surface—put 2 to 3 generous tbsp. of cheese mixture (or more depending on size of chicken breast) and roll up. Continue with rest of chicken breasts. Refrigerate at least 2 hours so filling will become firm and chicken easier to handle. Take 2 sheets of phyllo; butter one and place second one on top of it. Center 1 breast on phyllo about 2 inches from top; fold top over and fold sides in, rolling up breast in phyllo. (May be frozen at this point.) Butter tops and place on flat cookie sheet. Bake at 350° for 1 hour.

If there is remaining cheese and phyllo, cut phyllo

in half and butter as with chicken. Spoon cheese mixture (2 tbsp.) into phyllo and roll in same fashion. Butter and bake and serve as appetizer or freeze and serve in future.

Note: If phyllo becomes too brown during baking, cover with brown paper bag until done.

"Worth taking the time to prepare."

Linda Kaplan (Mrs. Steven)
M. S. Kaplan Company
Chicago, Illinois

TURKEY WALNUT

Preparation Time: 30 minutes
Cooking Time: 6 minutes

Serves: 4
Prepare Ahead
(partially)

1 tbsp. cornstarch
½ tsp. sugar
2 c. cooked slivered turkey
1 bunch green onions, cut into one inch lengths
1 c. walnut halves

¼ c. oil or melted shortening
½ c. turkey or chicken broth
3 tbsp. Worcestershire sauce
cooked rice

Combine cornstarch and sugar in a bowl. Add turkey, onions and walnuts; mix lightly. Heat oil very hot in skillet. Add turkey mixture; cook and stir 2 to 3 minutes until lightly browned. Add broth and Worcestershire sauce. Bring to a boil and simmer 2 to 3 minutes, stirring frequently. Serve on rice.

"This turns left-over turkey into an elegant entree."

Sherri Samuels
Midwest Steel Co., division of
H. Samuels Co.
Madison, Wisconsin

CHICKEN HOW-SO

Preparation Time: 15-20 minutes
   (estimated)
Cooking Time: 30 minutes

Serves: 4-6
Prepare Ahead

2 chicken breasts (1 lb.),
   skinned and boned
2 tbsp. butter or
   margarine
1 can golden mushroom
   soup
½ c. water
1 beef bouillon cube
1 tbsp. soy sauce
1 tsp. Worcestershire
   sauce
½ tsp. curry powder

1 8 oz. can bamboo shoots,
   drained
½ c. sliced celery
½ c. sliced onion
1 3 oz. can sliced
   mushrooms, drained
1 small green pepper, cut in
   strips
3 tbsp. dry white wine
½ tsp. poppy seed
1 3 oz. can chow mein
   noodles

Cut chicken into 1½ inch pieces. In medium skillet, brown chicken in butter or margarine until golden brown. Stir in the soup, water, bouillon cube, soy sauce, Worcestershire, curry, and poppy seed. Mix well. Cover and simmer 15 minutes, stirring occasionally. Add the bamboo shoots, celery, onion, and mushrooms. Cover and simmer 10 minutes or until tender-crisp. Stir in the green pepper and wine; cover and simmer 2 to 3 minutes more. Serve over chow mein noodles.

"A delicious make ahead meal for company or family."

Mrs. John Rodman (Mrs. John)
Rodman-Atlanta, Inc.
Lakeville, New York

SOUTH SEAS CHICKEN

Preparation Time: 1 hour
Cooking Time: 30 minutes

Serves: 4
Prepare Ahead
Freeze (except coconut)

1⅓ c. Minute Rice
½ tsp. salt
1⅓ c. boiling water
1 c. chopped celery
¾ c. sliced green pepper
¾ c. drained canned chunks of pineapple
3 tbsp. butter, melted
2 tbsp. flour

1 c. chicken stock
½ c. pineapple juice
2 tsp. soy sauce
⅛ tsp. pepper
½ tsp. salt
1½ to 2 c. diced cooked chicken
1 tbsp. lemon juice
1⅓ c. coconut

Prepare Minute Rice following directions on box for four servings. Saute celery, green pepper and pineapple chunks in butter about five minutes. Stir in flour. Add chicken stock, pineapple juice, soy sauce, pepper and ½ tsp. salt. Cook, stirring constantly, until mixture is thickened. Add chicken and lemon juice; heat thoroughly. Arrange on rice, sprinkle with coconut.

"Very good for buffets or large parties."

Peggy Soentgen (Mrs. Edward)
Aluminum Smelting & Refining Co., Inc.
Maple Heights, Ohio

BAKED BEEF TENDERLOIN

Preparation Time: ½ hour
Cooking Time: ¾-1 hour
Oven Temperature: 375°

Serves: 10
Prepare Ahead
Partially

1 whole beef tenderloin, trimmed to 4-5 lbs.
6 slices bacon, cut in half
1 green pepper
1 to 2 Bermuda onions

1 lb. mushrooms, sliced
2-3 tsp. butter or margarine
1 c. catsup
⅛ c. Worcestershire sauce
1 c. water

Lay tenderloin out flat; tail tucked under to make meat as even in thickness as possible. Assemble ingredients on top of filet in this order: bacon—criss-cross; onion—¼ inch horizontal slices; green pepper cut in ¼ inch julienne strips. Dot with butter. This can be assembled early in the day and refrigerated. Bring beef to room temperature before baking. Put beef in a roasting pan that will hold it comfortably. Cover whole tenderloin with 8 oz. catsup, Worcestershire sauce. (If you are at the end of the catsup bottle, put water in it to rinse out, and pour water into bottom of pan.) Bake at 375° for 45 minutes to 1 hour, depending on thickness of meat. Baste every 15 minutes with water and juices in pan. Remove from oven when meat thermometer registers lower than the rareness you want. Meat will continue to cook as it sits. Meanwhile, cook sliced mushrooms with 1 tsp. butter in top of double boiler for ½ hour, stirring once or twice, so they draw their own juice. Add ½ tsp. Kitchen Bouquet for color.

When beef is cooked, pour pan juices and any vegetables, bacon, that may have fallen off, into the mushrooms and you have the gravy. Slice and serve.

"Eye of round may be substituted when market is depressed."

Marilyn Hirchhorn (Mrs. Joseph)
David J. Joseph Co.
Cincinnati, Ohio

COLD OR HOT MARINATED BEEF TENDERLOIN

¾ c. honey
¼ c. lemon juice
½ c. soy sauce
½ c. Worcestershire sauce
1 stick oleo (I use Diet
  Mazola)

1 package Lipton's Onion
  Soup Mix
Beef tenderloin

Mix first 4 ingredients to make marinade. Pierce beef tenderloin on each side, pour marinade all over and refrigerate overnight.

Preheat oven to 350°. Make a paste of oleo and onion mix; rub on top of meat. Place beef in shallow baking pan; pour marinade over meat; bake for 15 to 20 minutes basting periodically.

Remove meat from oven and place on grill at medium heat. Continue basting with drippings from pan as well as marinade. Turn roast once as you would a steak. Do not overcook.

Slice into individual filets and serve hot or slice and serve cold with red horseradish sauce:
½ c. mayonnaise
½ c. red mayonnaise

For parties slice tenderloin into thin slices and serve with party size twist rolls.

Sylvia Berman (Mrs. Fred)
Berman Bros.
Birmingham, Alabama

BEEF & MUSHROOMS IN OYSTER SAUCE

Preparation Time: 20 minutes
Cooking Time: 5 minutes

Serves: 4-6
Prepare Ahead
Freeze

1 lb. flank or top round steak, partially freeze and slice into ⅛" thick pieces, about 2" long
3 small white onions, sliced thinly
2 c. small button, fresh mushrooms, clean and drain
1 medium size green pepper, chopped

Sauce
¼ c. beef stock or bouillon
⅓ c. oyster sauce (available in oriental section in supermarket)
1 tbsp. soy sauce
¼ c. dry Vermouth
1 tbsp. cornstarch

Combine sauce ingredients. Pour mixture over meat slices and marinate overnight. Heat fry pan, add ½ tsp. oil and add onions, and green pepper. Stir fry with wood spatula for 2 minutes; remove onion mixture and set aside. Heat remaining oil and add meat mixture. Stir fry approximately 2 minutes. Add button mushrooms and stir in quickly. Add onion mixture and cook for 1 minute. Serve hot with rice pilaf or baked potato. Delightful with a good red wine.

"Beef, mushroom mixture with delicate flavor made by oyster sauce."

John T. Kossakoski
Enterprise Company
Santa Ana, California

CHINESE MEATBALLS

Preparation Time: 30 minutes, including cooking time

Serves: 4
Prepare Ahead
Freeze

Meatballs
1 lb. ground beef
¾ c. celery
¼ c. chopped almonds
1 clove garlic
1 tsp. salt
½ c. fine dry bread
  crumbs
1 tbsp. soy sauce
½ tsp. monosodium
  glutamate
2 eggs, slightly beaten
cornstarch
3 tbsp. oil

Sauce
½ c. sugar
3 tbsp. cornstarch
1 c. chicken broth
½ c. vinegar
½ c. pineapple juice
2 tsp. soy sauce
½ c. green pepper, cut into
  strips
1 c. pineapple chunks

Mix meat, celery, almonds and garlic with salt. Add bread crumbs, soy sauce, monosodium glutamate and eggs. Form into balls about 1 inch. Roll in cornstarch. Brown on all sides in hot oil. Simmer about 15 minutes, turning frequently. Mix sugar and cornstarch together. Add chicken broth, vinegar, soy sauce and pineapple juice and cook, stirring constantly until smooth and thick. Add green pepper and pineapple and heat through. Pour over meatballs and serve on rice.

"A pungent, different oriental dish."

Martha Rossen (Mrs. Bernie)
Lefton Iron & Metal
East St. Louis, Illinois

MEATBALLS AND CABBAGE

Cooking Time: 3 hours
Oven Temperature: 350°

1½ lb. hamburger
1 medium cabbage
spices
1 medium onion, finely
   chopped

1 bottle chili sauce
1 can cranberries
1 tbsp. brown sugar
water

Mix hamburger, spices and onion as if for meat loaf. Form meat balls. Slice cabbage. Grease casserole; place layer of cabbage on bottom of casserole; add layer of meat balls; top with remaining cabbage. In separate bowl mix chili sauce, cranberries, brown sugar and 1 chili bottle of water. Pour sauce over casserole and bake covered in 350° oven for 2 hours. Remove cover and bake an additional hour. Serve over rice.

Yale Davis
West End Iron & Metal Corp.
Duluth, Minnesota

MOTHER'S CHILI

Preparation Time: 1 hour
Cooking Time: 45 to 55 minutes

Serves: 6
Prepare Ahead
Freeze

2 lbs. extra lean ground
  beef or ground round
  (do *not* use regular chili
  beef)
1 large onion
1½ to 2 packages
  Williams Chili
  Seasonings

1 clove garlic, crushed
2 8 oz. cans tomato sauce
1 can cold water
dash salt
dash sugar

In 4 qt. heavy pot with tight lid, brown very finely chopped onion and crushed garlic in very small amount of oil. Add meat and brown. Drain all grease from pan (IMPORTANT). Add remaining ingredients. Cover; cook over low heat about 45 minutes. Stir once or twice.

*Beans optional. If added, cook only 10 minutes.

"Enchiladas, guacamole salad and light fruit dessert compliment this chili recipe."

Charlene Segal (Mrs. Sam H.)
J. L. Proler Iron & Steel
Houston, Texas

CINCINNATI CHILI

Preparation Time: Very minimal
Cooking Time: 4 hours total

Serves: 8
Prepare Ahead
Freeze

1 qt. water
2 lbs. ground beef
2 med. onions, finely
  chopped
2 8 oz. cans tomato sauce
5 whole allspice
½ tsp. crushed red pepper
1 tsp. ground cumin seed
4 tbsp. chili powder

½ oz. unsweetened baking
  chocolate
4 cloves garlic, minced
2 tbsp. cider vinegar
1 large bay leaf
5 whole cloves
2 tsp. Worcestershire sauce
1½ tsp. salt
1 tsp. cinnamon

Place beef in a 4 qt. pot, add water and stir until beef separates to a fine texture. Boil slowly for 30 minutes. Add remaining ingredients. Stir and bring to a boil. Reduce heat and simmer, uncovered, for about 3 hours. Pot may be covered the last hour after the desired consistency is reached. Chili should be refrigerated overnight so the fat can be lifted off before re-heating. Delicious served over spaghetti, topped with grated cheese and grated onion. May be served with hot dog on bun with cheese, onion, and mustard.

"Delicious spicy warm dish that is perfect for cold nights or after football parties."

Mary Ann Bloom
  (Mrs. Lawrence)
Scrap Corp. of America
Northbrook, Illinois

GRANDMA'S STUFFED CABBAGE ROLLS IN SOUP

Serves: 6
Prepare Ahead

Cabbage Rolls
1 large head cabbage

Soup
5 c. water
left over cabbage, cut up
1 tsp. sour salt
2 tbsp. brown sugar
1 can (8 oz.) tomato sauce
1 onion, sliced
meat bone (opt.)

Stuffing
2 lb. lean ground beef
1 tsp. salt
dash of pepper
1 onion, greated
¼ c. matza meal or raw rice
1 egg (opt.)

Boil tea kettle of water. Tear cabbage head and cut off top of core. Place in large, heavy pot, core side up and pour the boiling water over it. Steam in covered pot for 10 minutes. Rinse in cold water and carefully remove 12 to 14 leaves, one at a time. Slice off thick part of vein on each leaf to make them more pliable. Drain on paper towel.

Start soup by cleaning same pot. Take left over cabbage and cut in pieces. Add water, sour salt, sugar, tomato sauce, onion and bone. Bring to a boil.

To make stuffing, mix beef, salt, pepper, onion and matza meal together. Place large spoonful of mixture onto a cabbage leaf near cut off end and turn up that end over mixture; then turn both sides to the middle and roll tightly. Repeat until 12 to 14 rolls are made. Place them carefully into the boiling soup open side down (toothpicks may be used to hold rolls together). Reduce heat and simmer for 1 hour.

"A meal in a pot."

Sylvia Landau (Mrs. Bernard)
M.S. Kaplan Co.
Chicago, Illinois

TINA'S SPAGHETTI

Preparation Time: 20 minutes
Cooking Time: 6-8 hours—sauce
*   15 minutes—meatballs*
Oven Temperature: 350°—meatballs

Serves: 8
Prepare Ahead
Freeze

Sauce
¼ c. olive oil
1 large onion, chopped
1 lb. Italian sausage,
   chopped
½ lb. pepperoni, sliced
1 28 oz. can tomatoes,
   chopped
1 28 oz. can tomato puree
1 16 oz. can tomato paste
1 bay leaf
soup bone (optional)
⅛ c. sugar
1½ tsp. salt
1½ tsp. pepper
1½ tsp. garlic powder
1 tsp. oregano

Meatballs
2 lbs. ground beef
1 c. dry bread crumbs
   (Italian)
¼ c. olive oil
¼ c. water
2 eggs, well beaten
½ c. Romano cheese
1 tsp. garlic powder
1 c. minced parsley
½ tsp. salt
2 tsp. pepper

Sauce   Brown onion and chopped sausage in olive oil. Add remaining ingredients. Stir and cook over low heat for 6-8 hours.

Meatballs   In a bowl combine all ingredients. Mix well and form into balls. Bake at 350° for 15 minutes.

Combine sauce and meatballs and serve over pasta.

"Tasty and easy."

Anne Murray (Mrs. Walter)
Luria Bros.
Houston, Texas

SPAGHETTI SAUCE

Preparation Time: 35 minutes
Cooking Time: 3 hours or all day in a
crock pot

Serves: 12
Prepare Ahead
Freeze

2 lbs. ground round
1 15½ oz. can whole
tomatoes
2 15½ oz. cans tomato
sauce
2 15½ oz. cans tomato
puree
1 small can tomato paste
1 can tomato soup
3 tbsp. grated Parmesan
cheese

½ tsp. garlic powder
approximately 1 tsp. each of
the following ingredients
(more or less according to
taste):
oregano
chili powder
sweet basil
1 bay leaf
1 onion, chopped

In a large kettle saute onion in small amount of oil. Add ground round and cook until browned. Pour off fat. Add all the remaining ingredients and cook on low heat for approximately three hours. Serve over cooked spaghetti or macaroni. May also be cooked all day in a crock pot.

"Tasty sauce to be served over various pasta products."

Elaine Bielniak
Intermetal U. S., Inc.
Cleveland, Ohio

OVERNIGHT BEER BARBECUED COUNTRY RIBS

Preparation Time: 2 hours day before, 1
hour day of serving
Cooking Time: 2 hours at most

Serves: 6-8
Prepare Ahead

2 small onions, chopped fine
1 box dark brown sugar
2 tbsp. lemon juice
½ tsp. fresh ground pepper

2 bottles Open Pit Bar-B-Q Sauce
1-2 cans of beer
6-8 lbs. country ribs, sliced individually by butcher

Combine all of the above ingredients except ribs to make beer barbecue sauce. The day before your barbecue place your ribs in a large saucepan and barely cover with water, bring to a boil and simmer covered for 40 minutes to 1 hour, or until tender. Place in pre-made barbecue sauce in large bowl and place in refrigerator overnight. Grill the pre-cooked country ribs over medium coals, basting with the barbecue sauce frequently for 30 minutes or until ribs are tender and browned. Weber or other smoker type grill preferred. Remove from grill and serve.

"Can be made ahead so that the hostess can meet and greet her guests."

Janet Ireland
Marco Steel Supply Co.
Champaign, Illinois

SAUERBRATEN

Cooking Time: 3 to 4 hours
Oven Temperature: 350°

Serves: 6 to 8
Prepare Ahead

6 lbs. beef roast—cover
  with brine of:
1 pt. white vinegar
3 tbsp. pickling spice
1 tsp. whole allspice
2 or 3 cloves
½ tsp. whole pepper

3 tsp. salt
1 large onion, cut-up
2 or 3 bay leaves
1 tbsp. brown sugar
water to cover roast

Let roast stand 3 or 4 days (longer if possible). Remove from liquid; reserving liquid. Roast in oven until tender, adding liquid as needed. Remove from liquid; slice or cut in pieces. Strain liquid and add about 12 ginger snaps to thicken gravy. Warm meat in gravy.
Optional: add ½ pt. of whipping cream to gravy.
Suggestion: serve with wide noodles.

"Midwestern style of sweet & sour roast."

Annabelle Loeb (Mrs. Archie)
Loeb Metal Recycling Co.
Watertown, Wisconsin

MEAT LOAF

Preparation Time: 20 minutes
  (estimated)
Cooking Time: 1¾ hours
Oven Temperature: 325°

Serves: 12
Prepare Ahead
Freeze

2 lbs. ground chuck
1 lb. ground pork
2 garlic cloves, finely
  chopped
1 lg. onion, finely chopped
1 tsp. salt
1 tsp. black pepper

1 bay leaf, crumbled
½ tsp. thyme leaves,
  crumbled
1 tsp. green pepper, chopped
½ c. dry bread crumbs
2 eggs
bacon

Mix all ingredients except bacon thoroughly and knead with the fingers until the mixture is thoroughly blended. Form into a long loaf or cake and press firmly. Arrange enough slices of bacon on the bottom of a baking pan to hold the meat loaf. Brush loaf with butter and cross with 2 to 4 additional slices of bacon. Roast at 325°, basting occasionally, for 1½ to 1¾ hours, or until the meat loaf is cooked through. Basting often makes a moister loaf. If served hot, let stand on hot platter 10 to 15 minutes before carving, to settle juices. Also serve with topping consisting of mixture of catsup, mustard, brown sugar and honey to cover loaf, which would be put on the last half hour of cooking.

"A new delicious tasty recipe for meat loaf."

Mary Ears Bathe (Mrs. Gene)
Moble Auto Crushers Corp.
Grand Prairie, Texas

LIVERKNAEFLY
(LIVER DUMPLINGS)

Preparation Time: 45 minutes
Cooking Time: 5 minutes

Serves: 10-12
Prepare Ahead
Freeze

½ c. yearling beef liver
4 eggs
¼ c. onion
½ c. fresh chopped
  parsley
¾ tsp. allspice

¾ tsp. nutmeg
¼ tsp. ground cloves
¾ tsp. black pepper
1 tsp. salt
4 c. flour
water or milk for liquid

Cut liver in pieces and put in blender, along with eggs, onion and other spices. Blend well, add parsley, blend again for a short time so bits of green are still visable. Put in bowl, add flour, water or milk and work dough. Dough will be soft and sticky. Put on plate or small cutting board and cut into small pieces with long sharp paring knife. Place pieces into salted boiling water. Dumplings are finished when they float to the top. (5 minutes) Strain dumplings and drain, removing to another pot. Can reuse water for more. Season finished product with bacon grease or gravy. Broth can be used for reheating.

"A wonderful tasty compliment for chicken, roast beef or pork."

Virginia Shapiro (Mrs. Earl)
Shapiro Brothers Scrap Iron &
  Metal
Festus, Missouri

STUFFED BREAST OF VEAL

Preparation Time: 1 hour
Cooking Time: 2½-3 hours
Oven Temperature: 325°

Serves: 10
Prepare Ahead
Freeze

4-5 lb. veal breast
salt
1 medium onion, finely
chopped
2 tbsp. oil

2 tbsp. parsley, minced
1 small can mushroom
pieces and stems (reserve
juices)
1 c. brown rice

Have pocket cut in veal breast. Wipe with damp towel and sprinkle with salt inside and out. Cook rice with 1 tsp. salt in 3 cups boiling water. Let stand over medium heat until rice is tender, 25 minutes. Saute onion in oil until soft but not brown. Mix rice, onion, mushrooms and juice. Correct seasoning. Fill the veal breast pocket with above mixture. Close pocket with skewers or large toothpicks. Place breast side down in roasting pan and bake uncovered in 325° oven for 2½-3 hours until tender. Baste with accumulated liquid.

"Delicious, ethnic type of entree."

Lillian R. Wessel (Mrs. Sam)
Hyman Michaels Co.
Chicago, Illinois

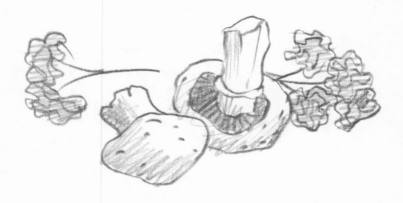

VEAL SCALLOPINE WITH WINE

Preparation Time: 1 hour
Cooking Time: 15 minutes

Serves: 8
Prepare Ahead
Freeze (better if not)

2 lbs. thinly sliced, trimmed veal, pounded
½ c. Parmesan cheese
3 tbsp. flour
½ c. butter
1 tbsp. olive oil
1½ c. sliced fresh mushrooms

½ c. chopped scallions
1 c. diced green pepper
1 c. dry white wine
½ c. dry sherry
4 beef bouillion cubes
salt
pepper
garlic salt

Cut veal into individual serving pieces. Season with salt, pepper and garlic salt. Dredge with mixture of Parmeasan cheese and flour. Saute veal until golden brown in a mixture of ¼ c. butter and olive oil. Remove veal from pan and keep warm.

In a second pan saute until just tender, mushrooms, scallions and green pepper in ¼ c. butter. Remove from heat.

Place veal and vegetables in a dutch oven. Mix wine, sherry and bouillion cubes. When cubes are dissolved, pour mixture over veal and vegetables. Cover and simmer for 15 minutes.

Remove to serving platter and garnish with parsley. Serve with green noodles tossed with butter, sour cream and Parmesan cheese.

"A delicate blend of flavor and texture."

Francine Rifkin (Mrs. Larry)
Rifkin Scrap Iron & Metal Co.
Saginaw, Michigan

ROUMANIAN BAKED LEG OF LAMB & VEGETABLES
(GEVHECHI CU CARNE)

Preparation Time: ½ to ¾ hour
Cooking Time: 3 hours
Oven Temperature: as noted in procedure

Serves: 8 plus
Prepare ahead as noted in procedure
May be frozen but dish loses characteristic quality

3 large potatoes, sliced ¼" thick
3 large onions, sliced ¼" thick
1½ c. washed long grain rice
1 head cauliflower, separated
1 eggplant, approx. 2 lbs., peeled and cut in 1" cubes
1 can (2 lb. 2 oz.) plum tomatoes

1 c. frozen peas
¾ c. water
1 leg of lamb, 7-8 lb.
1 clove garlic, slivered
1 tsp. ground ginger
2 tsp. salt
1 tsp. freshly ground pepper
2 tsp. sweet paprika
1 tbsp. rosemary, whole or ground
2 tbsp. margarine

Line bottom of roasting pan with ⅔ of the potatoes, covered by ⅔ of the onions. Cover with 1 cup of rice, the can of tomatoes (cut tomatoes in half crossways), juice of tomatoes, cup of peas and the cauliflower. Layer with remaining potatoes and onions. Add ¾ cup of water. Sprinkle with 1 teaspoon of salt and ½ teaspoon of pepper. Dust with 1 teaspoon of paprika.

Remove all but a thin layer of top fat from the lamb. Cut as many slits as you have garlic slivers and insert into lamb. Rub with rosemary and dot with margarine. Place lamb on vegetables, surround with remaining rice and cover. Bake in preheated 400° oven for 1 hour. Reduce oven to 300° and bake for an additional hour. Remove lid and bake for ¾ hour. Turn off heat and leave in unopened oven ¼ hour. Total 3 hours in oven.

The lamb should have a nice crust. May be reheated uncovered at 250° before serving.

Recommend serving with cold dill pickles, sour tomatoes, sauerkraut and other relishes.

"A zesty and colorful combination of meat and vegetables."

Peg Landesberg (Mrs. Arnold)
Lindemann of America, Inc.
Havertown, Pennsylvania

BARBECUED LEG OF LAMB

Preparation Time: 1 hour   *Serves: 8 to 10*
Cooking Time: 40 to 50 minutes

**7 to 8 lb. leg of lamb
    (boned & butterflied by
    butcher)
1 clove garlic, crushed
¾ c. oil
¼ c. red wine vinegar
½ c. chopped onion
2 tbsp. Worcestershire
    sauce**

**1 bay leaf, crushed
3 tsp. Dijon mustard
    (prepared)
2 tsp. salt
½ tsp. basil
½ tsp. oregano
⅛ tsp. black pepper
½ tsp. celery salt
½ tsp. dry mustard**

Place lamb in shallow pan, fat side down. Mix rest of ingredients and pour over lamb. Cover tightly and refrigerate overnight, turning several times. Remove meat from refrigerator 2 hours before cooking. Cook meat 20-25 minutes per side on medium high charcoal or gas grill. Baste several times with marinade. Remove, slice and serve with pepper jelly. Meat will be medium on the ends and medium rare in the middle.

**Anne Wilson (Mrs. Robert)
Wilson Scrap Service Inc.
Birmingham, Alabama**

LAMB SHANK SUPREME

Preparation Time: 10-15 minutes   *Serves: 2*
Cooking Time: 1½-2 hours   *Prepare Ahead*
Oven Temperature: 350°

2 lamb shanks   **2 tbsp. margarine, melted**
¼ c. Italian salad dressing   **Pam**
½ c. dry red wine

Mix together salad dressing and wine. Pour over lamb shanks and allow to marinate for 2-4 hours. Spray small roaster with Pam. Add lamb shanks, marinade and margarine.

Allow to roast at 350° for 1½-2 hours basting frequently.

"A rich tasting lamb, tender and special."

JuDeane Luntz, (Mrs. Andrew)
Luntz Corporation
Columbus, Ohio

SALMON LOAF

Preparation Time: 5 minutes   *Serves: 6*
Cooking Time: 45 minutes
Oven Temperature: 350°

3 eggs   **1 large can salmon, drained**
2 carrots   **½ stick of butter**
1 onion   **bread crumbs**
½ c. milk

Melt ½ stick of butter in pan. Place eggs, carrots, onion, milk, and salmon in blender and mix. Pour salmon mixture into buttered pan and sprinkle bread crumbs on top. Bake in 350° oven for 45 minutes.

"Wonderful and easy luncheon dish."

Mildred Graff (Mrs. Reuben)
Scrap Comp. of America
Chicago, Illinois

SHRIMP de JONG

Preparation Time: 30 minutes   *Serves: 6 people*
Cooking Time: 15 minutes   *Prepare Ahead*
Oven Temperature: 400°   *Freeze*

**2½ lbs. medium to large
   shrimp, cleaned and
   deveined
1 16 oz. can unseasoned
   breadcrumbs
¾ lb. butter or margarine,
   softened
4 lg. garlic cloves,
   pressed**

**2 tbsp. minced parsley
   (fresh or dried)
½ tsp. salt
pinch of tarragon
pinch of marjoram
1 tbsp. lemon juice
   concentrate
¼ c. dry vermouth**

Beat butter with wire whip until light and fluffy. Add the bread-crumbs, garlic, parsley, seasonings, lemon juice and vermouth. Form into ball. The texture of mixed crumbs and seasonings and butter should be more grainy than buttery. If necessary, add more crumbs to make grainy. Place cleaned and deveined shrimp in either a glass pyrex dish (if dish is to be served as a casserole) or in individual scallop shells (if it is to be served as an appetizer). A scallop shell can hold about 8 to 12 shrimp. Shrimp should be laid out flat rather than piled up. Slice the ball of butter and crumbs into sections and lay in ⅛ inch layers over all the shrimp in either the shell or the pyrex dish. Bake at 400° (after preheating) for about 15 minutes or until the topping is melted and the shrimp are cooked. The dish can be prepared in advance and frozen before baking or kept in refrigerator for several hours before baking. Cover with foil while storing before baking; thaw dish partially, if frozen, before placing in oven, or adjust cooking time.

"A finely seasoned succulent baked shrimp dish."

**Audrey Chanen (Mrs. Philip)
Chanen's Inc.
Quincy, Illinois**

LOBSTER (OR SHRIMP) OLD FRENCH MARKET STYLE SERVED OVER ORANGE RICE

Preparation Time: 30 minutes
Cooking Time: 25 minutes

Serves: 2
Prepare Ahead
(reheat in double boiler)

Lobster
4 small white onions, peeled
4 small mushrooms (deeply gash at ⅛" spaces)
2 tbsp. butter
1 medium lobster, meat only (or ½ lb. shrimp)
1 tbsp. minced onion
⅛ tsp. salt
1 black peppercorn
3 tbsp. burgundy wine
1 tsp. tomato paste
1 tbsp. flour
1 cube beef bouillon
1 small fresh tomato, peeled and chopped
1 spray parsley, chopped
¼ clove garlic, minced
¼ tsp. dried thyme
1 bay leaf
few drops A-1 Sauce

Orange Rice
2 tbsp. butter
⅓ c. diced celery with leaves
1 tbsp. minced onion
1 tbsp. grated orange rind
½ c. orange juice
¾ c. water
½ c. rice

Simmer white onions 15 minutes in small covered saucepan using 1 tbsp. butter. Add mushrooms, cook 2 minutes more and set aside. To 1 tbsp. butter melted in saucepan, add minced onion, lobster, salt and peppercorn. Simmer covered 2 minutes. Add wine and tomato paste and cook until wine is almost absorbed; sprinkle on flour; add beef bouillon, stirring until just thickened. Add remaining ingredients including mushrooms and onions; simmer 3 minutes. Cook rice according to panel on rice box.

"Quick, easy and elegant."

Carol Behn (Mrs. John)
CNA Insurance
Chicago, Illinois

CLAMS GUISSEPPE

Preparation Time: 20 minutes   *Serves: 10*
                                            Prepare Ahead

2 cans minced clams   **2 tbsp. basil**
1 large can chopped   **2 tbsp. oregano**
**   mushrooms**   **1½ lbs. spaghetti or linguini**
1 lb. margarine   **   noodles**
6 cloves garlic

Heat clams and mushrooms in own juice. In separate pan, melt butter. Add spices and garlic to butter for sauce. Cook spaghetti as directed on box. Drain clams and mushrooms and add to butter mixture. Pour over drained spaghetti or linguini.

"This is a rich pasta and sauce."

Rosemarie Surath
(Mrs. Bernard)
L. Surath and Sons Scrap Iron &
**   Metal**
Bay City, Michigan

JEAN'S SHRIMP CREOLE

Preparation Time: 30 minutes
Cooking Time: 65 minutes

Serves: 8
Prepare Ahead
Freeze

Heaping tbsp. lard
Heaping tbsp. flour
2 onions, chopped
2 stalks celery, chopped
2 cloves garlic, chopped
1 green pepper, chopped
2 tsp. parsley
Large can tomatoes (28 oz.), crushed

¼ c. vermouth or dry white wine
1 large bay leaf
¼ tsp. thyme
½ tsp. cayenne pepper
2 tsp. Worcestershire sauce
salt—to taste
2 lbs. raw, shelled shrimp

Heat the lard in large heavy kettle. Add flour and cook until nicely browned. Add vegetables and cook until brown. Add crushed tomatoes with juice, Vermouth, and all seasonings. Cook sauce about 1 hour. Add shrimp and cook about 5 minutes or until pink and done. Serve with rice which is cooked separately.

"A great party recipe and very simple to prepare."

Jean Rosenthal (Mrs. Richard)
The Purdy Company
Madison, Illinois

BUNNY'S CRAB IMPERIAL

Preparation Time: 20 minutes
Cooking Time: 15 minutes
Oven Temperature: 350°

Serves: 4
Prepare Ahead
Freeze

4 tbsp. butter	**1 pimiento, minced**
1½ tbsp. flour	**1 tbsp. onion, minced**
⅓ tsp. dry mustard	**1 lb. lump crabmeat**
dark cayenne pepper	**¼ c. sherry**
1 c. half & half	**grated cheese**
¼ c. mayonnaise	**paprika**
2 tbsp. capers (optional)	**salt**

Melt 2 tbsp. butter in saucepan. Stir in flour, mustard, cayenne pepper. Cook until slightly brown. Add half & half, stirring over low heat until creamy and smooth. Stir in mayonnaise, pimiento, capers (if desired). Add small amount of salt if desired. Stir in the sherry. Keep sauce over hot water. Melt remaining butter in skillet. Add onions. Simmer until soft. Add crabmeat and stir very carefully with fork until slightly brown. Pour warm sauce over crabmeat being careful not to break up lumps. Spoon into individual shells or 5 inch au gratin dishes. Sprinkle with cheese (about 1 tbsp. per serving) and a little paprika. Bake in 350° oven for 15 minutes.

"Easy but elegant."

Helen Richman (Mrs. Benjamin)
S. D. Richman Sons
Philadelphia, Pennsylvania

ITALIAN SAUSAGE AND PEPPERS MARINARA

Preparation Time: 1 hour maximum
Cooking Time: 1 hour

Serves: 6
Prepare Ahead
(Peppers and
tomatoes can
be chunked in
advance)
Freeze

**2 lbs. sweet Italian
  sausage links
5 large green bell peppers
5 large tomatoes, whole**

**Italian blend spice
Lemonade mix (or sugar and
  lemon juice)**

Saute sausages in 12 inch deep skillet or dutch oven until brown on all sides. Remove and slice into 1 inch chunks on angled bias (it is quicker to cut a number of them at a time). Saute rough cut or wide julienned peppers in small residue of sausage drippings after having poured out most of the fat. While they cook, chunk tomatoes, then add to peppers, cooking both slowly. Drain any fat from the sausages and then add to pan. As tomatoes cook down to sauce add spice to taste, approximately a few teaspoons but variable due to amount of spice in sausage. Continue to cook, mashing remaining pieces of tomatoes for smoother sauce. Add lemonade mix to taste. Adjust final taste with a little more spice.

"Chunked sweet Italian sausage sauteed with green peppers, marinara style."

**Philip Chanen
Chanen's Inc.
Quincy, Illinois**

RICE-CHEESE-CHILI CASSEROLE

Preparation Time: 20 minutes
Cooking Time: 45 minutes
Oven Temperature: 350°

Serves: 6-8
Prepare Ahead
Freeze

1 c. rice
1 lb. cheddar cheese, grated
1 lb. Monterrey Jack cheese, grated

1 4 oz. can diced ortega chilies
1 cube butter
1 pt. sour cream

Steam rice according to package directions. Then mix together with remaining ingredients. Place in a shallow Pyrex baking dish. Top with some additional grated cheese, if desired. Bake in 350° oven for 45 minutes.

"The combination of rice, cheese and chilies is excellent, making for a good accompaniment with beef and pork."

> Susan Daniels (Mrs. Alan)
> K & D Salvage Co.
> Bakersfield, California

PRISNJAC

Preparation Time: 6 minutes
Cooking Time: 40 to 50 minutes
Oven Temperature: 350°

Serves: 8
Prepare Ahead
Freeze

6 eggs
½ c. butter
½ lb. grated cheddar cheese
1 pkg. chopped frozen spinach

6 tbsp. flour
2 1 lb. cartons cottage cheese

Cook and drain frozen spinach. Add other ingredients and mix well in large bowl. Place in one 9" x 12" glass pan or two 8" x 8" glass pans and bake 40 to 50 minutes in 350° oven, until set.

"Terrific for lunch, brunch or supper."

> Dorothy M. Prober (Mrs. David)
> DeKalb Iron & Metal Co.
> DeKalb, Illinois

CHEESE MUSHROOM PUFF

Preparation Time: 30 minutes
Cooking Time: 30 minutes
Oven Temperature: 375°

Serves: 6 to 8
Prepare Ahead

¾ lb. fresh mushrooms, sliced
2 onions, sliced
3 tbsp. butter
2 c. milk
3 eggs, separated

1 c. grated cheddar cheese
½ tsp. salt
dash of pepper
4 matzos, broken in chunky pieces

(For a variation you may use broccoli or spinach, chopped, instead of mushrooms, if they are fresh. Add them uncooked. If frozen, thaw and drain thoroughly.) Saute mushrooms and onions in butter; set aside. Heat milk below boiling point, add cheese, salt and pepper to milk; blend well. Beat egg yolks. Add some of the hot milk mixture to egg yolks; mix well; then return all to milk mixture, stirring constantly. Fold mushrooms and onions into milk-cheese mixture. Fold in matzos. Beat egg whites stiff, but not dry. Fold into cheese mixture. Pour mixture into greased 7" x 12" baking dish and bake at 375° for 30 minutes or until knife comes out clean.

"Fantastic——Delicious."

Libbie Wool (Mrs. Sam)
General Iron & Salvage Co.
St. Louis, Missouri

SAVORY EGGS

Cooking Time: 45-50 minutes
Oven Temperature: 325°

Serves: 12
Prepare Ahead

2 c. grated American cheese
¼ c. butter
1 c. light cream or half & half

½ tsp. salt
¼ tsp. pepper, freshly ground
2 tsp. prepared mustard
12 eggs, slightly beaten

Spread the cheese in a greased 13 x 9 x 2 baking dish. Dot with butter. Combine the cream, salt, pepper and mustard. Pour half of this mixture over the cheese. Pour eggs into the baking dish. Add the remaining cream mixture. Bake in moderately slow oven (325°) until set, about 45 minutes.

"Recipe can be cut in half."

Esther Marks (Mrs. Irwin)
Steel City Iron & Metal, Inc.
Youngstown, Ohio

ENTREES

BAKED CHEESE FONDUE

Preparation Time: 10-20 minutes
Cooking Time: 1-1¼ hours
Oven Temperature: 350°

Serves: 4
Prepare Ahead
Freeze before
* baking*

12 oz. mild cheddar
  cheese
8 slices of white bread
1½ lbs. fresh mushrooms,
  sauteed or 1 can
  mushrooms

3 eggs
2 c. milk
½ tsp. salt
½ tsp. dried mustard
  powder
dash pepper

Cut crust off bread and slice into cubes. Slice cheese. Saute mushrooms if using fresh mushrooms. Mix egg, milk, salt, mustard and pepper together. Place ingredients into casserole dish in the following order: bread, mushrooms, cheese and repeat. Cover the top completely with cheese. Pour egg mixture into dish. Cover and let set overnight. Bake uncovered at 350° for 1-1¼ hours.

"Mild cheese flavored dish which is excellent for buffet brunch or luncheons."

Elyse Zelunka (Mrs. Alan)
Gensco Equipment
Toronto, Ontario
Canada

95

COMMON ABBREVIATIONS

Teaspoon .... tsp. or t.
Tablespoon .... tbsp. or T.
Cup .... c.
Pint .... pt.
Quart .... qt.
Gallon .... gal.
Ounce .... oz.
Pound .... lb.
Hour .... hr.
Minute .... min.
Medium .... med.
Package .... pkg.
Envelope .... env.
Square .... sq.
Margarine .... marg.
Monosodium Glutamate .... M.S.G

Vegetables

MUSHROOM SUPREME

Preparation Time: 15 to 20 minutes
Cooking Time: 30 to 45 minutes
Oven Temperature: 350°

Serves: 9 to 12
Prepare Ahead
(up to baking)

1½ to 2 lbs. whole fresh
mushrooms
2 beef bouillon cubes
½ c. hot water
½ stick butter or
margarine

2 tbsp. flour
½ c. cream or milk
⅛ tsp. salt
dash pepper
½ c. bread crumbs
extra butter or margarine

Clean mushrooms. Remove stems and cut into pieces. Saute mushrooms in butter until browned. Dissolve beef bouillon in hot water. Melt ½ stick butter and blend with flour. Add cream, salt, pepper and beef broth. Combine mushrooms and flour mixture. Top mixture with cheese and bread crumbs and bake in buttered casserole for 30 to 45 minutes in 350° oven.

Janet Cohen (Mrs. Ken)
Cohen Brothers, Inc.
Middletown, Ohio

SPINACH-CHEESE PIE WITH NO ROLL CRUST

Preparation Time: 20 minutes
Cooking Time: 75 minutes
Oven Temperature: 375°

Serves: 8 (recipe
can be
doubled)
Prepare Ahead
Freeze

Filling
6 eggs
2 10 oz. pkg. frozen
chopped spinach
16 oz. shredded
Mozzarella cheese
12 oz. cottage cheese
⅛ tsp. pepper
¼ tsp. garlic powder
½ tsp. salt

Pastry & Topping
2 c. all-purpose flour
1 tsp. salt
¾ c. shortening

Filling Cook spinach and drain well. Mix remaining ingredients with cooked spinach and fill pastry. Sprinkle with topping and bake. Allow to stand 10 minutes before serving.

Pastry In medium bowl, with pastry blender, mix flour, salt and shortening until coarse crumbs. Reserve ¾ c. for topping. Sprinkle remaining dough with 2 to 3 tbsp. cold water a tbsp. at a time until pastry is moist enough to stick together. Press into 9" pie pan and fill.
"Wonderful side dish for any meal."

> **Linda Cole (Mrs. Jeffrey)**
> **Alport Scrap & Salvage Co.**
> **Detroit, Michigan**

ROASTING PAN BEANS

Preparation Time: 15 minutes
Cooking Time: 1 hour
Oven Temperature: 350°

Serves: 8 to 10
Prepare Ahead
Freeze

1½ to 2 lbs. small link port sausages
1 can (16 oz.) kidney beans (drained & washed)
1 can (16 oz.) lima beans (drained & washed)
2 cans (16 oz. each) pork & beans (juice & all)
1 can (16 oz.) green beans (strained)

1 can tomato soup (rinse out with 1 can of water)
½ c. catsup
½ c. barbecue sauce
1 c. onions sauteed in 2 tbsp. butter and 1 tbsp. fresh mustard

Cook sausages in small amount of water. Then brown and cut each link into 5 pieces. Mix all beans in large roaster. Add all other ingredients except sausages and mix gently. Add sausages. Bake covered for one hour at 350°.
"Good buffet casserole."

> **Ruth Szarka (Mrs. George)**
> **Aluminum Smelting & Refining**
> **Maple Heights, Ohio**

FRESH VEGETABLES QUICHE

Preparation Time: 1 hour
Cooking Time: 40 minutes
Oven Temperature: 325°

Serves: 4

1 medium onion, thinly
  sliced
1 green pepper, chopped
1 garlic clove, crushed
1 tsp. salt
½ tsp. pepper
½ tsp. marjoram
3 tbsp. butter
5 eggs
2 c. cheddar cheese,
  finely diced (about 8
  oz.)

4 c. fresh mixed vegetables,
slightly cooked to tender-
crisp state, cut into bite
size pieces (suggested
vegetables are broccoli,
green beans, carrots,
zucchini, cauliflower, etc.)

1 pie crust, regular or whole
wheat

Bake pie crust for 15 minutes at 350°. Saute onion, green pepper and garlic in butter until soft. Remove mixture from heat and cool slightly. Beat eggs until frothy; stir in sauteed vegetables, cheese, salt, pepper, marjoram and cooked vegetables. Pour mixture into crust. Bake in 325° oven until center is firm (about 40 minutes.) Let stand 10 minutes before serving.

"A pie full of cheese and fresh vegetables. Can also be served as an appetizer or entree."

Cathy Bush (Mrs. Eddie)
Martin Bush Iron & Metal Co.
Minneapolis, Minnesota

BROCCOLI CHEESE CRUNCH

Preparation Time: 15 minutes
Cooking Time: 20 minutes
Oven Temperature: 350°

Serves: 6
Prepare Ahead

2 10 oz. pkgs. frozen
  chopped broccoli
1 8 oz. pkg. Velveeta
  cheese

1 c. butter or margarine
20 Ritz Crackers

Melt butter in frying pan. Crush crackers with rolling pin to a very coarse consistency. Stir until butter and crumbs are thoroughly mixed. Set aside. Prepare 2 pkgs. broccoli as directed on package. Drain. Cut cheese into cubes and mix broccoli and cheese into 9" square cooking dish. Top with additional cracker crumbs. Bake in greased 9" square Corningware or pyrex dish at 350° for 20 minutes or until bubbling.

"Very easy vegetable in cheese sauce with tasty topping."

Janet Brady (Mrs. James)
Brady Iron & Metal Co., Inc.
Newark, New Jersey

BROCCOLI CASSEROLE

Preparation Time: 15 minutes *Serves: 8*
Cooking Time: 1 hour *Prepare Ahead*
Oven Temperature: 350°

6 unbeaten eggs
2 lbs. small curd cottage cheese
6 tbsp. flour
½ lb. processed cheese (Velveeta), diced

1 pkg. frozen chopped broccoli, (not cooked)
¼ lb. butter
2 green onions, chopped (tops and all)

Thaw frozen broccoli quickly by placing in colander and running hot water over it. Then separate the pieces with a fork and drain well. Have all the ingredients at room temperature. In order listed, layer ingredients in a large bowl of an electric mixer. Beat until well blended. Pour into a greased 9" x 12" baking dish and bake at 350° for 1 hour, or until a knife comes out almost clean. It should be golden brown and bubbly on top. Let set at room temperature 10 minutes before serving.

"Souffle-like consistency—no hint of vegetable content."

Joan Pielet (Mrs. Sam)
Pielet Brothers Trading, Inc.
Des Plaines, Illinois

DELICIOUS SPINACH

Preparation Time: 15 minutes
Cooking Time: 30 minutes
Oven Temperature: 350°

Serves: 10
Prepare Ahead

4 10 oz. pkgs. chopped frozen spinach
½ c. butter or margarine, melted
2 8 oz. pkgs. cream cheese
1 8½ oz. can artichokes, drained and quartered

1 6 oz. can water chestnuts, drained and thinly sliced
1½ tsp. onion powder
salt and pepper to taste
seasoned bread crumbs
⅓ c. grated Parmesan cheese

Cook spinach in boiling salted water until defrosted. Drain and squeeze out excess moisture. Add butter, cream cheese, artichokes, water chestnuts, onion powder, salt and pepper to spinach and mix thoroughly. Put into greased 2 qt. baking dish. Cover with seasoned bread crumbs and Parmesan cheese. Bake in 350° oven for 30 to 40 minutes until very hot.

"This is a delicious but easy 'gourmet' recipe."

Arleen Dobkin (Mrs. Stanley)
Shapiro Sales Company
St. Louis, Missouri

CARROT RING

Preparation Time: 15 minutes
Cooking Time: 30 minutes
Oven Temperature: 350°

Serves: 8
Prepare Ahead
Freeze

1 c. Crisco
½ c. brown sugar
1½ c. grated carrots (grate on large side of 4-way grater)
2 eggs, separated

½ tsp. salt
1 c. flour
1 tbsp. lemon juice & rind
½ tsp. soda
1 tsp. baking powder

Cream Crisco and sugar. Add egg yolks. Sift dry ingredients together. Add to mixture. Add grated carrots, lemon juice and rind. Add beaten egg whites. Bake in small, greased, 6" ring mold. Very pretty to serve with frozen peas in the center.

"A light delightful way to eat carrots."

Charlotte Kasle (Mrs. Louis)
Kasle Brothers
Flint, Michigan

SUMMER GARDEN CASSEROLE

Preparation Time: 20 minutes   *Serves: 12*
Cooking Time: 1½ hours   *Prepare Ahead*
Oven Temperature: 350°

3 c. green beans, trimmed & cut

2 c. yellow summer squash, sliced

2 c. zucchini, sliced

2 c. tomatoes, quartered, then halved

1 c. rice (long grain fancy)

¼ to ½ c. onion, chopped fine

½ c. green pepper, chopped fine

1 10¾ oz. can Campbell's chicken broth

4 tbsp. butter

Season to taste with basil, salt and pepper

Wash each vegetable carefully and prepare as above. Combine all ingredients and mix well. Place in buttered 3 qt. covered casserole. Preheat oven to 350° and bake for 45 minutes. Remove from oven and gently mix to insure even cooking. Return to oven for an additional 45 minutes of cooking.

"Appetizing to the eye as well as to the palate."

Denise S. Luntz (Mrs. Thomas)
Luntz Corporation
Warren, Ohio

103

CHEESE SCALLOPED CARROTS

Cooking Time: 35 to 45 minutes
Oven Temperature: 350°

Serves: 8
Prepare Ahead—
refrigerate until
¾ hour before
baking
Freeze

12 medium carrots, pared
and sliced
¼ c. butter or margarine
1 tsp. salt
2 c. milk
¼ tsp. celery salt
½ lb. American cheddar
cheese or Velveeta
cheese

3 c. buttered soft bread
crumbs
1 small onion, minced
¼ c. all-purpose flour
¼ tsp. dry mustard
⅛ tsp. pepper

Cook carrots covered in 1″ boiling salted water until barely tender; drain. Meanwhile, in saucepan, gently cook onion in butter for 2 to 3 minutes. To onion, stir in flour, salt and mustard; add milk. Cook, stirring constantly, until smooth. Add pepper and celery salt. In 2 qt. casserole, arrange layer of carrots, then layer of cheese. Repeat until all carrots are used, ending with carrots. Pour on sauce and top with bread crumbs. Bake in 350° oven for 35 to 45 minutes.

"Tender carrots in a creamy cheese sauce."

Sue Ann Kibiloski
Samuels Hide and Metal
Paragould, Arkansas

VEGETARIAN DELIGHT
(Microwave)

VEGETABLES

Preparation Time: 10 minutes
Cooking Time: 20 minutes

Serves: 6 to 8
Prepare Ahead

- 1 large eggplant, peeled & sliced
- 1 medium green pepper, cut into strips
- 1 large onion, sliced
- ¼ tsp. garlic powder
- 3 tbsp. oil
- 1 16 oz. can tomato wedges, drained
- 2 tsp. minced parsley
- ½ lb. cottage cheese
- ½ lb. fresh spinach, washed, drained & torn (or 1 10 oz. box frozen spinach, thawed)

- ½ lb. sliced Mozzarella cheese
- 1 8 oz. can tomato sauce
- ½ tsp. oregano (or ½ tsp. Italian Seasoning)
- ½ tsp. sugar
- Dash onion salt
- ½ c. grated Parmesan cheese

In 2 qt. flat casserole, place eggplant, green pepper, onion, garlic powder, and oil. Cover with wax paper or plastic wrap. Microwave on high for 10 to 12 minutes or until eggplant is tender. Add tomato wedges and parsley to mixture and microwave for 2 to 3 minutes on high. Layer cottage cheese, then spinach, then Mozzarella cheese. In small dish, mix tomato sauce with seasonings and Parmesan cheese and pour over casserole mixture. Microwave for 3 to 5 minutes on Level 5 (slow) just until cottage cheese is slightly melted.

"Tasty one dish cheese and vegetable casserole for complete meal."

Phyllis Dumes (Mrs. Stanley)
Dumes, Inc.
Vincennes, Indiana

LAYERED VEGETABLE LOAF

Cooking Time: 75 minutes
Oven Temperature: 300°

Serves: 8 to 12
Prepare Ahead
(bake same
day as serving)

Spinach Layer
2 pkgs. (10 oz. each)
frozen spinach, thawed
or 2 c. cooked fresh
spinach
1 egg
⅛ tsp. nutmeg
salt—to taste (about ¾
tsp.)
1 tbsp. whipping cream or
milk as needed

Carrot Layer
3 c. sliced raw carrots,
about 1 lb.
1 egg
2 tbsp. brown sugar
salt—to taste, about ¾ tsp.
1 tbsp. whipping cream or
milk, as needed

Cauliflower Layer
2 pkgs. (10 oz. each)
frozen cauliflower or
about 3 c. cooked
cauliflower
1 egg
salt—to taste, about 1 tsp.
3 tbsp. whipping cream or
milk, as needed

Spinach Layer Drain spinach and puree in blender or processor with remaining ingredients, adding as much milk or cream as necessary to make it smooth. The puree must be moist, but not runny. Drain, if necessary. Set aside.

Cauliflower Layer Cook cauliflower until tender. Drain and follow directions as for spinach. Set aside.

Carrot Layer Cook carrots until tender. Drain. Follow directions as for spinach.

To assemble   Preheat oven to 300°. Butter 9″ x 5″ loaf pan well. This is of the utmost importance. Be sure you can see a film of butter all over. Spread carrot mixture evenly over bottom of loaf pan, then spread cauliflower evenly over carrot layer, then spread spinach evenly over cauliflower layer. Cover the top with oiled or buttered wax paper. Set in a shallow 9″ x 13″ pan of boiling water (1 to 2 inches deep) and bake at 300° for 1 hour, 15 minutes. Test for doneness by gently lifting paper and jiggling loaf to see if it is firm. It may take up to an half an hour longer. Remove loaf and wait 10 to 15 minutes. Remove paper and run knife around the sides. Unmold by putting the serving plate on top of the loaf and inverting. Gently lift off the loaf pan. Serve hot or cold. To serve, slice loaf into slices. The vegetable loaf may be served with lightly Sauteed Tomatoes (recipe follows) if desired.

SAUTEED TOMATOES

3 medium sized ripe
  tomatoes, cut into 1″
  cubes (approx. 2 c.)
3 tbsp. butter
1 clove garlic, finely
  chopped

½ tsp. dried basil
1 tsp. sugar
¼ tsp. salt
⅛ tsp. freshly ground black
  pepper

Cut the tomatoes into 1″ cubes and place them in a collander or strainer to drain. Chop the garlic either by hand or in a food processor, fitted with the steel blade. If using a processor, drop the garlic down the feed tube while the motor is running. In a medium skillet, melt the butter over medium heat, add the chopped garlic, and saute until it is soft, but not brown, about 1 minute. Add the drained tomatoes and the rest of the ingredients and saute just until the tomatoes are hot. Do not overcook or the tomatoes will disintegrate.

"Vegetable loaf also can be served cold as an appetizer."

Lois Hollander (Mrs. Edward)
Philipp Brothers
Skokie, Illinois

EGGPLANT CASSEROLE

Preparation Time: 1 hour   *Serves: 8*
Cooking Time: 1 hour
Oven Temperature: 350°

2 lbs. eggplant, peeled
  and cubed
3 c. boiling water
4 tbsp. melted butter
1 c. milk
4 eggs
6 oz. tomato sauce
1 tsp. Worcestershire
  sauce
6 oz. mushroom soup, not
  diluted
4 tbsp. flour

2 c. cornflake crumbs
1 lb. ground chuck
1 tbsp. salt (or to taste)
½ tsp. black pepper
½ tsp. dried mint
½ tsp. parsley flakes
½ tsp. garlic salt
2 tbsp. pimento, chopped
1 large onion, grated
¼ c. bell pepper, grated
3 stalks celery, grated
2 stalks carrots, grated

Cook eggplant in boiling water for about 10 minutes or until tender. Drain and put in large mixing bowl. Beat eggs and blend in milk, tomato sauce, and butter. Add to mixing bowl; stir well. Add soup, flour and 1 c. cornflake crumbs (reserve 1 c.); stir well. Separate meat and add to bowl together with salt, pepper, Worcestershire sauce, dried mint, parsley flakes, garlic salt. Mix well. Add pimento, onion, bell pepper, celery and carrots. Mix well. Pour into greased 10" x 14" x 3" pyrex baking dish and top with the 1 c. reserved cornflake crumbs. Bake in preheated 350° oven for 1 hour or until golden brown.

"Tasty eggplant casserole."

Mrs. William Thomas
Southern Scrap & Metal Co.
Meridian, Mississippi

EGGPLANT PARMESAN

Preparation Time: 30 minutes
Cooking Time: 30 minutes
Oven Temperature: 350°

Serves: 6
Prepare Ahead

1 large eggplant
½ c. flour
2 tsp. salt
½ tsp. pepper
4 tbsp. olive oil, divided
usage (you may use a
little more oil to saute
eggplant)
1 medium onion, thinly
sliced

2 cloves garlic, minced
3 medium tomatoes,
chopped
¼ tsp. leaf basil, crushed
1 9 oz. pkg. Mozzarella
cheese, sliced
½ c. grated Parmesan
cheese

Cut eggplant into crosswise slices 1" thick; dip in water to wet surface. Mix flour, 1 tsp. salt and ¼ tsp. pepper in shallow dish. Dip eggplant into flour mixture to coat lightly. Use 2 tbsp. olive oil in large frying pan to saute eggplant, turning once, until brown on both sides. Remove to an oiled 2 qt. casserole dish. Add remaining 2 tbsp. oil to same frying pan and saute onion and garlic until soft. Stir in tomatoes, salt, pepper and basil; cook until thickened. Top eggplant with Mozzarella cheese, sprinkle Parmesan and top with tomato sauce. Bake in 350° oven for 30 minutes or until cheese is melted and eggplant is tender.

"Very easy to prepare and tastes like pizza."

Evelyn Clark (Mrs. James)
Chaparral Steel Co.
Midlothian, Texas

COMPANY NOODLE PUDDING (SWEET)

Preparation Time: 15 minutes　　　　*Serves: 10 to 12*
Cooking Time: 45 minutes　　　　　*Prepare Ahead*
Oven Temperature: 350°　　　　　　*Freeze*

1 lb. broad noodles
　(cooked)
1½ pts. sour cream
1½ c. melted butter
1½ c. sugar
1 tsp. vanilla
2 1 lb. cans crushed
　pineapple, drained

5 eggs, beaten
1 pkg. dried apple slices
1 pkg. dried apricots, cut
　into small pieces
extra sugar
cinnamon

Grease 12" x 16" dish that can be used oven-to-table preferably.
Place apple slices on bottom of pan. Mix all other ingredients
together. Pour over apple slices. Top with mixture of cinnamon
and sugar. Bake at 350° for about 45 minutes.
"Excellent dish for brunch or buffet table."

Bernice Mahler (Mrs. Donald)
Morrow Steel Company
Detroit, Michigan

SPICED NOODLE PUDDING

Preparation Time: 30 to 45 minutes　　　*Serves: 8 to 12*
Cooking Time: 35 to 40 minutes　　　　*Prepare Ahead*
Oven Temperature: 350°　　　　　　　*Freeze*

4 eggs
16 oz. creamed cottage
　cheese
1 c. commercial sour
　cream
¼ c. sugar
1 tsp. salt
2 tsp. cinnamon
½ tsp. pure vanilla extract
2 c. apple, pared and
　diced

1 c. raisins
8 oz. medium-wide egg
　noodles, slightly
　undercooked and drained
2 tbsp. butter or margarine
1 c. cornflake crumbs
¼ c. slivered, blanched
　almonds
extra sour cream
½ tsp. nutmeg

In a large mixing bowl, beat eggs slightly; add cottage cheese, sour cream, sugar, salt, cinnamon, nutmeg and vanilla; beat gently—just until ingredients are evenly distributed. Add apples, raisins and noodles; stir together well. Pour into a buttered shallow (12 x 8 x 2) baking dish. In a small skillet, melt butter; remove from heat and stir in crumbs and almonds; sprinkle over noodle mixture. Bake in a preheated 350° oven until topping is golden or about 35 to 40 minutes. Let stand at room temperature 10 minutes before serving, but serve warm, with extra sour cream.

"A delicious accompaniment to beef or chicken entrees but can also be served as a dessert."

Alice Wamsley (Mrs. W. H.)
Wamsley Associates, Inc.
Media, Pennsylvania

NOODLE PUDDING

Preparation Time: 20 minutes   *Serves: 12*
Cooking Time: 1 hour   *Prepare Ahead*
Oven Temperature: 350°

1 lb. wide noodles
½ lb. butter or margarine, melted
1 pt. sour cream
1 lb. creamed cottage cheese

1 c. sugar
1 tsp. salt
2 8 oz. cans sliced yellow cling peaches, drained and cut-up

Preheat oven to 350°. Cook noodles according to directions on package. Drain and add to melted butter. Mix the buttered noodles with the sour cream, cottage cheese, sugar, salt and peaches which have been blended together. Pour into 3 qt. casserole and bake uncovered for 1 hour at 350°.

"Creamy, smooth not too sweet noodle pudding—always a hit!"

Patricia S. Caplan (Mrs. George)
Grant Steel Corporation
Pittsburgh, Pennsylvania

111

POTATO SWISS BAKE

Preparation Time: 1 hour
Cooking Time: 30 to 45 minutes
Oven Temperature: 350°

Serves: 6
Prepare Ahead
Freeze

4 to 6 large baking
   potatoes
½ lb. bulk Swiss cheese
caraway seed
3 large onions

salt
pepper
paprika
¼ lb. butter

Parboil potatoes in salted water. Meanwhile, saute sliced onions in butter, adding salt and dash of pepper. Grease bottom and sides of 2 qt. baking dish. Peel and slice potatoes. Alternate layers of potatoes and sauteed onions, sprinkling each layer with caraway seeds and small amount of salt and pepper. Spread each layer with slices of Swiss cheese. Sprinkle casserole lightly with paprika. Bake for 30 to 45 minutes until bubbly in 350° oven.

"Our family and friends adore this tasty casserole."

Velia Samuels (Mrs. Thomas)
H. Samuels Co.
Portage, Wisconsin

POTATOES GRATINES WITH BEER

Preparation Time: 20 minutes
Cooking Time: 1 to 1½ hours
Oven Temperature: 325°

Serves: 4 to 6
Prepare Ahead
Freeze

2 lbs. boiling potatoes (about 6 to 7 c.)
2 c. yellow onions, thinly sliced
butter
1 c. beer

1 c. beef bouillon (canned beef bouillon or 3 beef cubes)
2½ c. shredded Swiss cheese (imported)
salt and pepper

Cook the onions in a frying pan in butter until tender but not browned. Peel potatoes, wash them and slice them about ⅛ inch thick. Drain them on a paper towel thoroughly. Butter a fireproof baking serving dish (about 10 inches diameter and 2 inches deep). Spread half of the sliced potatoes in the baking dish. Over them spread half of the onions, and over the onions spread half of the cheese. *Salt very lightly* and pepper. Repeat another layer with the rest of the potatoes, then the onions. Salt very lightly and pepper. Combine the beer and bouillon and pour the mixture in dish (liquid should come almost to top layer). Spread the rest of the cheese. Dot with small pieces of butter and place the dish in the upper third of preheated oven (325°). Bake approximately 1 to 1½ hours or until potatoes are tender, liquid has been absorbed and top is nicely browned. Remove from oven, let stand 5 to 10 minutes, and serve.

"Scalloped potatoes with beef bouillon and cheese and beer."

Delphine Schiavone
(Mrs. Michael)
Michael Schiavone & Sons, Inc.
North Haven, Connecticut

WILD RICE CASSEROLE

Preparation Time: 45 minutes to 1 hour
Cooking Time: 25 minutes
Oven Temperature: 350°

Serves: 8
Prepare Ahead
    (up to baking)

**6 o. box Uncle Ben's Wild
    and Long Grain Rice**
1 medium onion, chopped
½ c. celery, chopped
**¼ lb. fresh mushrooms,
    sliced**

**¼ c. water chestnuts or
    toasted almonds, coarsely
    chopped**
1 stick butter
chicken or beef broth

Cook rice according to package directions (do not use seasoning package in box.) Also, substitute ½ of required water with chicken or beef broth. Saute onions, celery and mushrooms in butter. Add water chestnuts or almonds to rice and combine with saute mixture. Pour into 2 qt. casserole. Cover and bake for 25 minutes at 350°.

"Excellent accompaniment to beef and poultry dishes."

**David Witherspoon, Jr.
David Witherspoon, Inc.
Knoxville, Tennessee**

RICE RISOTTO

Preparation Time: 15 minutes
Cooking Time: 45 minutes

Serves: 8
Prepare Ahead
Freeze

1 large onion, cut small
¼ lb. butter (1 stick)
**¼ lb. prosciutto (Italian
    ham)**
2 c. uncooked rice

1½ qts. chicken broth
1 c. grated Parmesan cheese
1 small jar mushrooms
salt & pepper, to taste

Brown onion in butter until softened. Add prosciutto (which has been cut up into small bits); cook for 5 minutes. Add uncooked rice and blend together until golden brown. Add hot chicken broth a little at a time, until rice has absorbed most of the liquid (approximately 20 minutes). Add salt, pepper, mushrooms and cheese; mix well. Remove from burner, cover pot for 15 minutes, stirring occasionally until all broth is absorbed.

"A tasty dish that can be served with any meal."

Mary Avagliano (Mrs. Peter)
Schiavone-Bonomo Corp.
Jersey City, New Jersey

MAMA'S MEXICAN RICE

Preparation Time: 30 minutes
Cooking Time: 30 minutes

Serves: 4 to 6
Prepare Ahead
Freeze

1 c. long grain rice (quick-cooking rice not recommended)
2 tbsp. chicken fat (Schmaltz)
1 small onion, chopped fine

1 large, ripe tomato, peeled and chopped fine (approximately 1 c.)
2 c. water or chicken broth
1½ tsp. salt
pepper—to taste

Wash rice and drain. Fry rice in chicken fat until light brown, stirring constantly. Add onion and cook until onion is clear. Add tomato, salt, pepper; let cook a few minutes. Add boiling water or chicken broth to cover rice. Stir well. Cover with tight-fitting lid and cook on very low fire *without stirring* approximately 25 minutes, or until fluffy and tender.

"Delicious with roast beef or fowl, as well as with traditional Mexican food."

Thelma S. Lipsitz
M. Lipsitz & Co., Inc.
Waco, Texas

WHEN YOU MUST IMPROVISE

Baking powder (1 teaspoon) = ¼ teaspoon soda + ½ tsp. cream of tartar

Milk (1 cup) = ½ cup evaporated milk + ½ cup water

Sour milk (1 cup) = 1⅓ tablespoons vinegar + sweet milk to make 1 cup

Sour cream (1 cup) = 1 tablespoon vinegar + 1 cup evaporated milk or add vinegar to cottage cheese and blend

Chocolate (1 ounce) = 3½ tablespoons cocoa + 1 tablespoon butter

Corn syrup (1 cup) = 1 cup sugar plus ¼ cup liquid

Butter or margarine (1 cup) = ⅞ cup shortening + ½ teaspoon salt

Onion (1 small) = 1 tablespoon instant minced onion

Catsup or chili sauce for cooking (1 cup) = 1 cup tomato sauce + ½ cup sugar and 2 tablespoons vinegar

Thickening for gravies = instant potatoes

Desserts

CHOCOLATE FRENCH SILK

Preparation Time: 1 hour
Cooking Time: 15 to 20 minutes
Oven Temperature: 350°

Serves: 16 to 20
Prepare Ahead (2
*   to 3 days)*
Freeze

Crust
½ c. brown sugar
1 c. flour
½ c. chopped pecans
¼ c. margarine
¼ c. butter

Topping
1 pt. whipping cream
¼ c. confectioners sugar
instant coffee powder, to
   taste (optional)

Filling
1 c. butter
1½ c. sugar
1 tsp. vanilla
3 packets Nestle's Choco-
   Bake
4 eggs

Crust   Mix brown sugar, flour and pecans. Cut in butter and margarine. Pack into baking pan (13" x 9" x 2" or two 8" pans) and bake for 15 minutes in 350° oven or until brown. Cool.

Filling   Cream butter and sugar; mix in vanilla, chocolate and then eggs, one at a time, beating 5 minutes after each egg is added. Pour into cooled crust and refrigerate 24 hours before serving.

Topping   An hour or so before serving, beat whipping cream until stiff. Stir in confectioners sugar and instant coffee to taste. Spread over chocolate mixture.

"A crunchy crust with a rich chocolate, smooth as silk gourmet's delight filling."

Marie Ratasepp
Joliet Railway
McCook, Illinois

PEACHES 'N' CREAM CHEESE PIE

Preparation Time: 15 minutes
Cooking Time: 10 minutes — crust
30 minutes — filling
Oven Temperature: 350°

Serves: 6 to 8
Prepare Ahead

Crust
16 graham crackers
3 tbsp. sugar
⅓ c. melted butter

Filling
3-3 oz. pkg. cream cheese
⅓ c. milk
2 eggs
⅓ c. sugar
¼ tsp. vanilla
2 c. sliced fresh or canned cling peaches

Crust Roll 16 graham crackers into crumbs. Add sugar and ⅓ c. melted butter or margarine; blend well. Pack into 9″ pie pan to cover bottom and sides. Bake at 350° for 10 minutes.

Filling Blend cream cheese that has been softened and milk. Add sugar, eggs and vanilla; beat with rotary beater or hand mixer until smooth. Place peaches (sliced) in pie shell, arranged evenly. Pour cheese mixture over peaches. Bake in moderate oven (about 350°) for 30 minutes. Garnish top with extra peach slices and lightly sprinkle with nutmeg.

"It's easy to prepare and looks very professional when garnished with pinwheel of peaches and nutmeg dusted."

Mitzi Sapper (Mrs. Gerald)
Markovits & Fox
San Jose, California

SWISS FUDGE PIE

Preparation Time: 20 minutes
Cooking Time: 30 minutes
Oven Temperature: 350°

Serves: 6 to 8
Prepare Ahead
Freeze

⅓ c. butter (⅔ stick)
3 squares unsweetened
   baking chocolate
4 eggs
3 tbsp. flour

3 tbsp. white Karo syrup
2 c. sugar
¼ tsp. salt
1 tsp. vanilla
1 unbaked 9-inch pie shell

In top of double boiler or over low heat, melt butter and squares of chocolate. Meanwhile, place eggs in mixing bowl and beat until light. Add flour, Karo syrup, sugar, salt and vanilla to eggs and beat. Add the chocolate mixture (slightly cooled) and mix thoroughly and pour into a 9″ pastry lined pie pan. Bake at 350° for 30 to 40 minutes or until top is crusty and filling is set but still somewhat soft inside. Do not overbake. If you like a softer center next time, use only 2 tbsp. flour. Top with whipped cream or vanilla ice cream.

"For chocolate lovers."

Verna Redard (Mrs. Ruben A.)
Keystone Consolidated
Industries
Peoria, Illinois

GRASSHOPPER PIE

Preparation Time: 30 to 60 minutes

Serves: 6 to 8
Prepare Ahead
Freeze

16 to 20 Oreo Cookies
6 tbsp. butter
1-7 oz. jar Marshmallow
   Creme
2 c. whipping cream

2 tbsp. creme de cocoa
2 tbsp. white creme de
   menthe
green food coloring
chocolate curls

Crush cookies and combine with melted butter. Pat into greased 9" pie pan. Chill.

Combine Marshmallow Creme with creme de cocoa and creme de menthe. Beat until smooth using a rotary beater. Beat whipping cream until fairly stiff. Fold into marshmallow mixture. Tint with food coloring. Fill pie shell. Decorate with chocolate curls. Freeze overnight. This must be served directly from the freezer. Texture and consistency of ice cream.

"A cool, refreshing dessert with the texture of ice cream."

Louise Warshauer
(Mrs. William)
Alchem Aluminum
Fort Wayne, Indiana

EASY COCONUT PIE

Preparation Time: 15 minutes　　　　*Serves: 6*
Cooking Time: 45 minutes　　　　　*Prepare Ahead*
Oven Temperature: 350°

2 c. sugar	**¾ c. buttermilk**
5 eggs	**1 tsp. vanilla**
1 stick oleo (melted)	**1 small can coconut**

Mix all ingredients and pour into two 9" pie crusts. Bake in 350° oven for 45 minutes.

Phyllis Hawk (Mrs. Clarence E.)
Klean Steel Manufacturing Co.
Pearl, Mississippi

BUTTER CRUNCH PIE CRUST*

Preparation Time: 30 minutes
Cooking Time: 15 minutes
Oven Temperature: 400°

Serves: 6 to 10
Prepare Ahead

To be used with coconut cream pie filling.

½ c. butter
¼ c. brown sugar
1 c. sifted flour

¾ c. chopped walnuts
¾ c. coconut, shredded

Pre-heat oven. Using a pastry blender, combine butter, brown sugar and flour. Add nuts and coconut and spread thinly on a jelly roll pan. Bake 15 minutes until lightly browned. Remove from oven and stir with a spoon to separate pieces. Set aside ¾ c. for topping and lightly pack browned ingredients into a 9" pie plate. Cool. As filling, make up your favorite recipe for coconut cream filling, using butter and "half and half" in the recipe. Pour this into the cooled shell, sprinkle with the ¾ c. topping and chill.

"An incredibly delicious dessert with an elusive and mysterious taste."

Annabel Custer
(Mrs. William R.)
Magnimet — Perrysburg
Perrysburg, Ohio

CHOCOLATE SURPRISE TORTE

Preparation Time: 45 to 60 minutes
Cooking Time: 10 minutes

Serves: 8 to 10
Prepare Ahead
Freeze

6 Hersheys candy bars (8 oz. medium)
1 pkg. large marshmallows (36)

1 pt. whipped cream
24 graham crackers
2 tbsp. butter

Crush graham crackers. Melt butter. Mix crackers and butter and press into spring bottom round torte pan, reserving ¾ c. In double boiler melt candy bars and marshmallows. Cool. Whip the cream and fold into the cool mixture. Put into graham cracker lined pan. Use reserved cracker crumbs to sprinkle on top. Put in freezer 24 hours. Take out of freezer 1 hour before serving.

"If you enjoy ice cream, this torte is cool, refreshing, delicious."

Sharon A. Thuecks
Miller Compressing Co.
Milwaukee, Wisconsin

ORANGE TORTE

Preparation Time: 10 minutes
Cooking Time: 25 minutes
Oven Temperature: 350°

Serves: 10
Prepare Ahead

Batter
1 box Duncan Hines
   Yellow Butter Cake Mix
4 eggs
1 c. oil
1 small can Mandarin
   oranges, do not drain

Filling
1 medium carton Cool Whip
1 pkg. vanilla instant
   pudding
1 medium can crushed
   pineapple, do not drain

Beat cake mix, eggs, oil and Mandarin oranges for 2 minutes. Pour into 2 greased 9" cake pans. Bake at 350° for about 25 minutes. Cool on rack for 15 minutes and remove from pans. Make filling by stirring all ingredients together. Spread filling between layers and on top. Trim with Mandarin oranges.

"Easy to make — good — tastes good."

Belle Peterman
Miller Compressing Co.
Milwaukee, Wisconsin

BUTTERSCOTCH TORTE

Cooking Time: 35 to 45 minutes
Oven Temperature: 350°

Serves: 10 to 12
Prepare Ahead
Freeze

Crust
20 Ritz crackers
1 c. chopped walnuts
1 tsp. baking powder
3 egg whites
1 c. sugar
1 tsp. vanilla
¼ tsp. salt

Filling
butter pecan ice cream

Sauce
⅔ c. brown sugar
⅔ c. white sugar
⅔ c. white Karo corn syrup
4 tbsp. butter
1 c. heavy cream

Crust   Crumble crackers. Combine with chopped walnuts and baking powder. Beat egg whites until stiff and gradually add 1 c. of granulated sugar, vanilla and salt. Fold two mixtures together and pour into 9″ or 10″ glass pie plate which is sprayed with Pam. Bake in 350° oven for 35 to 45 minutes or until golden brown. When cooled, crusts can be frozen. Recipe makes one Torte. Double the recipe and make 2 Tortes.

Filling   Take a third pie plate and butter. Cut 9″ circle of wax paper and place it in the buttered pie plate. Fill plate (on top of wax paper) with 1 pt. to 1 qt. of butter pecan ice cream. Place pan in freezer.

Sauce   Combine brown sugar, white sugar and corn syrup in saucepan. Bring to a boil, carefully. Add butter until syrup threads. Add heavy cream and bring to boil. Boil 3 minutes or until thick.

Assemble   Remove tortes and ice cream from freezer. Place ice cream between crusts. Slice torte and serve pieces topped with hot butterscotch sauce.

"Nutty confection with ice cream and luscious butterscotch sauce."

**Esther Schiavone
(Mrs. Joseph A.)
Michael Schiavone & Sons
North Haven, Connecticut**

LEMON CREAM TORTE

Preparation Time: 1 hour
Cooking Time: crust — 20 minutes
lemon filling — 15 minutes
Oven Temperature: 350°

Serves: 28
Prepare Ahead

Crust
1 c. flour
¼ lb. butter
2 tbsp. sugar
½ c. chopped walnuts

Second Layer
1-8 oz. pkg. cream cheese
¾ c. powdered sugar
1-6 oz. carton Cool Whip

Third Layer
2 pkgs. lemon pie filling (French's)

Top Layer
9 oz. Cool Whip
½ c. chopped walnuts

Crust Mix first four ingredients as for pie crust. Pat into 9" x 13" pan. Bake at 350° for 20 minutes. Cool.

Second Layer Beat together until smooth. Spread over cooled crust.

Third Layer Make third layer according to directions on box. Use only enough sugar for 1 box. Spread over cream cheese layer when slightly cool. (For variation use any flavor instant pudding mix — 2 pkgs. with 3 c. milk.)

Top Layer Spread whipped cream on top and sprinkle with chopped nuts. Cool for 2 hours. Torte will keep for 2 weeks.

"A light, delicious dessert, that looks fancy, but easy to make."

Carol Marrott
Merit Industries
Cleveland, Ohio

126

PINEAPPLE & WALNUT TORTE

Serves: 12 or
more
Prepare Ahead
Freeze

1 package (7½ oz.) vanilla
   wafers
1 c. butter or margarine
1 c. extra-fine granulated
   sugar

2 eggs
2 tsp. vanilla
2 c. drained, grated
   pineapple
1 c. finely chopped walnuts

Crush vanilla wafers into very fine crumbs. Makes about 2 cups. Cream butter to consistency of mayonnaise; add sugar gradually while continuing to cream. Add eggs one at a time, beating well after each addition. Add vanilla; mix well. Combine pineapple and walnuts; stir until well mixed. Line a 8" x 5" x 3" loaf pan with foil, leaving overhang so loaf can be lifted out easily. Press ½ cup crumbs on bottom of pan. Add about ¼ pineapple mixture, spreading evenly. Repeat until crumbs and pineapple mixture are used up, ending with latter. (Reserve about 2 tbsp. of crumbs to be scattered on top.) Chill 24 hours or longer, or freeze. I have kept torte frozen for months. No defrosting necessary; just slice from freezer as many portions as needed and within minutes, it is ready to eat.

"Delicious, very attractive and can always be on hand for unexpected company."

Rae Wodis (Mrs. Harvey)
McCabe Scrap Iron &
   Materials Co.
Galesburg, Illinois

STRAWBERRY-RHUBARB HALO

Preparation Time: 1 hour
Cooking Time: Cake: 15 minutes
Filling: 35 minutes
Oven Temperature: Cake: 425°
Filling: 375°

Serves: 8
Prepare Ahead
Freeze

Cake
2 c. flour
¼ c. sugar
1 tbsp. baking powder
¼ tsp. salt
¼ tsp. ground nutmeg
½ c. butter
2 eggs, slightly beaten
½ c. milk

Filling
1 lb. rhubarb (trim stalks,
cut into 1″ pieces; about
2½ c.)
⅔ c. sugar
1½ tbsp. cornstarch
1½ tsp. ground cinnamon
⅛ tsp. salt
1 pt. strawberries (hulled &
halved)

Halo
1 pt. heavy cream
½ c. confectioners sugar

Cake   In large bowl combine flour, sugar, baking powder, salt and nutmeg. Cut in butter until mixture resembles coarse crumbs. Add milk and eggs; stir until blended. Spoon into greased, wax-paper lined 8″ cake pan. Bake in preheated 420° oven about 15 minutes or until brown and cake tester comes out clean. Cool.

Filling   Place layer of rhubarb in buttered 2 qt. casserole. Combine sugar, cornstarch, cinnamon and salt. Sprinkle ½ over rhubarb. Add remaining rhubarb and sugar mixture. Mix well. Cover and bake at 375° about 30 minutes. Stir in strawberries. Cover and bake 5 more minutes. Chill.

Halo   Chill bowl and beaters. Beat cream and sugar until stiff.

Assemble   Cut cake in half crosswise. Fill with ½ of filling. Spoon halo around edge of top layer. Fill halo center with remaining filling. Chill until ready to serve.

Marie Capasso (Mrs. Frank)
Pascap Co., Inc.
Bronx, New York

ZUCCHINI-CREAM CHEESE CAKE

Preparation Time: 30 minutes
Cooking Time: 1 hour
Oven Temperature: 350°

Serves: 8 to 12
Prepare Ahead
Freeze

5 eggs, beaten
1⅛ c. oil
2¼ c. sugar
1½ tsp. grated lemon peel
¾ tsp. orange extract
½ tsp. vanilla
3 c. grated zucchini
3¾ c. flour

1¼ tsp. salt
¾ tsp. cinnamon
½ tsp. ginger
1½ tsp. soda
3 tsp. baking powder
¾ c. chopped walnuts
confectioners sugar
8 oz. pkg. cream cheese

Combine beaten eggs, oil and sugar. Beat well. Add lemon peel, orange extract, vanilla and zucchini. Beat well. In another bowl, combine flour, salt, cinnamon, ginger, soda and baking powder. Combine flour mixture with egg mixture. Add nuts and mix well. Pour into 2 greased and floured 9" x 5" loaf pans or small round "Dansk" pots. Bake in 350° oven for 1 hour. Cool until bread turns out. Cool on wire racks. Makes two loaves or two small round "cakes". Frost with cream cheese mixed with confectioners sugar. Sweeten to taste.

"Even our kids like it."

Priscilla Siskin (Mrs. Robert)
Siskin Steel & Supply Co.
Chattanooga, Tennessee

ITALIAN CREAM CAKE WITH CREAM CHEESE FROSTING

Preparation Time: 45 minutes
Cooking Time: 25 minutes
Oven Temperature: 350°

Serves: 8
Prepare Ahead
Freeze (without frosting)

Cake
1 stick butter
½ c. vegetable shortening
2 c. sugar
5 egg yolks
2 c. flour (all purpose)
1 tsp. soda
1 c. buttermilk
1 tsp. vanilla
1 small can angelflake coconut
1 c. chopped pecans
5 egg whites, beaten stiffly

Frosting
1-8 oz. pkg. cream cheese, softened
½ stick butter, softened
1 box powdered sugar
1 tsp. vanilla
chopped pecans

Cake   Cream butter and shortening. Add sugar and beat until smooth. Add egg yolks and beat well. Combine flour and soda. Add to creamed mixture alternately with buttermilk. Stir in vanilla. Add coconut and chopped nuts. Fold in stiff egg whites. Pour into three greased and floured 8″ pans. Bake at 350° for 25 minutes or until cake tests done. Cool and frost with cream cheese frosting.

Cream Cheese Frosting   Beat cream cheese and butter until smooth. Add sugar and mix well. Add vanilla. Beat until smooth. Spread between layers, on top and sides of cake. Sprinkle pecans between layers.

"A very rich, moist cake that will keep for a week in the refrigerator."

Sherry Landers
Klempner Brothers, Inc.
Louisville, Kentucky

CAROL'S CARROT CAKE

Preparation Time: 30 minutes　　*Serves: 12*
Cooking Time: 60 minutes　　　　*Prepare Ahead*
Oven Temperature: 350°　　　　　*Freeze*

Cake

2 c. sugar
1½ c. oil
2 tsp. vanilla
3 eggs at room
   temperature
2½ c. flour (whole wheat)
½ tsp. salt
1 tsp. baking powder

1 tsp. baking soda
1½ tsp. cinnamon
¾ tsp. ginger
¾ tsp. nutmeg
1 small can crushed
   pineapple, drained
2 c. finely grated carrots
1½ c. finely chopped pecans

Cream Cheese Frosting

1 stick (¼ lb.) butter
1-8 oz. pkg. cream cheese
1 box powdered sugar

1 tsp. lemon extract
grated lemon peel

Cake　With an electric mixer, beat together sugar, oil and vanilla. Add eggs one at a time, beating well after each addition. Sift together all the dry ingredients. Alternating with the flour mixture, add the remaining ingredients, beginning and ending with the flour mixture. Pour batter into two greased and floured 9″ cake pans. Bake at 350° (used a preheated oven) for 60 minutes. Check doneness with a toothpick. Let the layers cook in the pan for about 15 minutes; finish cooling on a cake rack.

Frosting　Let butter and cream cheese soften at room temperature; cream together with an electric mixer. Add sugar and vanilla and whip well. Spread on cooled cake. Sprinkle top of cake with grated lemon peel.

"A sinfully delicious cake."

Carol Newberger (Mrs. Mark)
Dallas Scrap Baling Co.
Dallas, Texas

LUSCIOUS LEMON POUND CAKE

Preparation Time: 30 minutes
Cooking Time: 1 hour, 45 minutes
Oven Temperature: 300°

Serves: 8 to 12
Prepare Ahead
Freeze

½ lb. butter
½ lb. Crisco
3 c. sugar
5 eggs
3 c. cake flour (do not sift)
¼ c. milk

½ tsp. baking powder
1 c. sour cream
1 tsp. vanilla
1 tsp. lemon extract
½ tsp. grated lemon peel

Cream butter, Crisco and sugar. Add eggs one at a time and beat well with electric mixer until mixture is light and fluffy. Add dry ingredients and continue to beat well. Add milk, vanilla and lemon and mix well. Gently fold in sour cream. Pour into greased and floured bundt pan. Bake. Let cook on rack 15 minutes before turning out. Let cool completely before serving.

"Delicious — moist — 'lemony' cake."

Deborah Anderton (Mrs. James)
Summit Steel Processing Corp.
Lansing, Michigan

EASY POUND CAKE

Preparation Time: 10 minutes
Cooking Time: 40 minutes
Oven Temperature: 350°

Serves: 12 to 15
Prepare Ahead
Freeze

2½ c. Presto
4 eggs, separated
½ lb. butter
½ c. milk

1¼ c. sugar
rind of 1 whole lemon
juice of ½ lemon

Beat egg whites until stiff. Combine butter, sugar, egg yolks, lemon rind and lemon juice. Add Presto and milk to mixture. Lastly, fold in beaten egg whites. Pour entire mixture into bundt pan and bake in 350° oven for 40 minutes or until cake tests done.

"Easy pound cake."

Susan Mayer (Mrs. Steven)
Philipp Brothers
New York, New York

MOCHA SPONGE CAKE

Preparation Time: 45 to 60 minutes   *Serves: 12 to 15*
Cooking Time: 1 hour
Oven Temperature: 325°

1 c. sugar
6 eggs, separated
2½ tbsp. strong coffee
¾ c. matzo cake flour

3 c. heavy cream, whipped
sugar to taste
coffee to taste

Beat egg whites until stiff and set aside. Beat egg yolks and sugar until light. Add coffee and cake flour last. Fold in stiffly beaten egg whites. Pour into spring form or tube pan. Bake about 1 hour in 350° oven. When done, invert cake on cake rack until cool. Split layers and fill with whipped cream with coffee flavoring and sugar to taste. Spread frosting on layers, on top and cover entire cake. Refrigerate a minimum of 6 hours. Even better served the next day. Note: cake may also be split into thirds and then filled and frosted.

"Light and delicious."

Amy Kerstein (Mrs. Robert)
Maryland Metals
Hagerstown, Maryland

ELLEN'S LAZY NO-BAKE LAYER CAKE

Preparation Time: 40 minutes

Serves: 12 to 16
Prepare Ahead
(tastes better)

2 to 3 commercially
  prepared pound cakes
1-6 ⅛ oz. pkg. instant
  chocolate pudding mix
½ pt. whipping cream
1 pkg. Hersheys mini
  chips

white creme de cacao (dark
  may be substituted)
1 to 2 tsp. sugar
water
milk

Prepare pudding as package directs. Set aside. Pour some creme de cacao into small pitcher (cream) and add water to create mixture—2 parts creme de cacao to 1 part water.

Line bottom of ungreased pan with very thin (¼") slices of pound cake. Pour creme de cacao over cake layer to moisten slightly. Add thin layer of pudding mixture. Sprinkle with chocolate chips. Repeat layers to top of pan ending with cake and creme de cacao.

Cover pan with plastic wrap and refrigerate for several hours or overnight.

To unmold, remove from refrigerator, run thin knife around edges of bowl or pan to loosen and invert into serving plate. Whip cream, sweetened to taste. Frost cake with whipped cream and sprinkle top with additional chips. Refrigerate until ready to serve.

"Delicious! Light! Liqueury!"

Ellen Neuberg (Mrs. Peter)
National Nickel Alloy Corp.
Pittsburgh, Pennsylvania

THAT CAKE

Preparation Time: 15 to 20 minutes   *Freeze*
Cooking Time: 50 to 60 minutes
Oven Temperature: 350°

Cake
4 eggs
¾ c. Mazola oil
¾ c. water
1 tsp. vanilla
1 tbsp. butter flavor
**   extract**
1 envelope (dry) Dream
**   Whip**
1 pkg. vanilla instant
**   pudding**
1 pkg. Duncan Hines
**   Deluxe II Yellow Cake**
**   Mix**

Streusel
½ c. sugar
2 tsp. cinnamon
2 to 2½ oz. chopped pecans
**   or walnuts**

Glaze
¾ c. powdered sugar
1 tsp. vanilla
1½ tbsp. milk
1 tsp. butter flavor extract

Beat all ingredients for cake for 7 minutes. Meanwhile, generously grease long angelfood cake pan (15½" x 5") with Spry up the sides and bottom. In small bowl, mix streusel ingredients. Spread ¾ batter in pan. Spoon ½ streusel mixture over, add remaining batter. Sprinkle remaining streusel over all. Marble slightly with knife. Bake width-wise. (Ends of pan almost touching sides of oven.) Cake will not turn out if baked ends front to back. Cool in pan. Do not invert pan for about an hour. Before removing from pan, run knife around edge, pushing to loosen. Gently turn over and remove from pan; immediately flip over so top side is up again (as it has baked). Mix ingredients for glaze and drizzle on top and down sides of cake.

"Delicious streusel coffee cake — named from happy exclamations of 'Oh, that cake'."

Joanie Levey (Mrs. Alan)
Alter Company
St. Paul, Minnesota

CHOCOLATE DATE CAKE

Preparation Time: 30 minutes　　　　*Serves: 15*
Cooking Time: 30 minutes　　　　　*Prepare Ahead*
Oven Temperature: 350°　　　　　　*Freeze*

½ c. butter	1 c. pitted dates
1 c. sugar	1 tsp. baking soda
2 eggs	1 tsp. vanilla
1¾ c. cake flour	1 c. boiling water
½ tsp. salt	1 pkg. chocolate bits
2 tbsp. cocoa	½ c. chopped nuts

Cut dates into small pieces. Put baking soda into boiling water and pour over dates. Cool. Sift dry ingredients together. Cream butter and sugar. Add eggs and vanilla. Beat. Add dry ingredients and date mixture alternately. Mix thoroughly. Spread in 9" x 13" greased pan. Sprinkle 1 small pkg. chocolate bits and chopped walnuts over top. Pat down. Bake in 350° oven for 30 minutes. (Do not overbake.)

"A delicious moist cake. Unusual because of the dates."

Muriel Reingold (Mrs. Jack)
Louis Levin & Company
Tonawanda, New York

BLUEBERRY BUTTER BUNDT CAKE

Preparation Time: 20 minutes　　　　*Serves: 10*
Cooking Time: 45 minutes
Oven Temperature: 325°

½ c. oil	butter cake mix (1 box)
3 eggs	1 15 oz. can blueberries
8 oz. package cream	(drained)
cheese	

Mix together oil, eggs and cream cheese. Add cake mix. Add blueberries. Bake in greased bundt pan at 325° for 45 minutes. Do not overcook.

"A very delicious, moist cake, yet very simple to prepare."

Marcy Johnson (Mrs. Dusty)
Tyler Pipe Industries
Tyler, Texas

YUM YUM CAKE

Preparation Time: 60 minutes
Cooking Time: 20 minutes
Oven Temperature: 350°

Serves: 30
Prepare Ahead
Freeze

1 yellow cake mix
2-3⅛ oz. packages vanilla
  instant pudding
2 c. milk
8 oz. cream cheese

9 oz. Cool Whip
1-20 oz. can crushed
  pineapple (well drained)
1 can coconut
1 c. chopped nuts

Bake yellow cake mix according to directions except pour onto a 15″ cookie sheet and bake at 350° for 20 minutes. Mix vanilla instant pudding with the milk; beat and set aside. Cream the cream cheese and Cool Whip; add pudding and beat until fluffy. Spread mixture on cool cake. To top, layer pineapple, coconut and nuts (in that order) on cake.

"Upon testing this cake your first words will be — 'yum yum'."

Judy Davis (Mrs. Robert)
Industrial & Rail Scrap, Inc.
Darlington, Pennsylvania

BANANA BUNDT CAKE

Cooking Time: 1 hour
Oven Temperature: 350°

Batter
1 pkg. Banana Cake mix
1 small pkg. instant
   banana pudding
4 eggs
½ c. oil
1 c. sour cream
2 large bananas, mashed
1-6 oz. pkg. chocolate chips

Sugar/Nut Mixture
¼ c. sugar
⅓ c. brown sugar
2 tbsp. cinnamon
½ c. chopped nuts

Grease bundt pan well. Pour half of batter in pan. Sprinkle sugar and nut mixture. Then add other half of batter. Bake 1 hour in 350° oven.

Mildred Kaplan (Mrs. Louis)
H.S. Kaplan Scrap Iron & Metal
Co., Inc.
St. Paul, Minnesota

POTATO CAKE

Preparation Time: 15 minutes
Cooking Time: 1 hour
Oven Temperature: 300°

Serves: 12 to 15
Prepare Ahead
Freeze

½ c. shortening
3 egg yolks
2 c. sugar
1 c. mashed potatoes
1 c. sour cream
1 tsp. baking soda

½ tsp. salt
¼ tsp. baking powder
2 tsp. cinnamon
2 c. flour
1 c. chopped pecans
1 c. cocoa

138

Cream shortening and egg yolks until fluffy. Add sugar and beat well. Add cocoa and mashed potatoes and blend well. Add sour cream, soda, salt and baking powder, blending to keep batter smooth. Add cinnamon and flour. Fold in beaten egg whites and add nuts. Grease and flour 10" tube pan. Bake in 300° oven for 1 hour.

"Keeps well and is better the second day."

> **Marguerite Hocking (Mrs. N.W.)**
> **Glick Iron & Metal Co.**
> **Jackson, Michigan**

CHERRY CAKE

Preparation Time: 20 minutes
Cooking Time: 45 to 50 minutes
Oven Temperature: 350°

Serves: 20
Prepare Ahead
Freeze

1½ c. sugar
1 c. butter
4 eggs
2 c. flour

1 tbsp. lemon juice or
  extract
1 can cherry pie filling
confectioners sugar

Gradually add sugar to butter; cream together until light and fluffy. Add eggs, one at a time. Beat well at low speed, add flour and lemon. Pour into greased jelly roll pan. Mark off 20 squares with a knife. Place 1 tbsp. cherry pie filling in center of each square. Bake at 350° for 45 to 50 minutes. While warm, sift confectioners sugar on top. Cool and cut.

"Mouth-watering, easy to prepare and extremely impressive to serve."

> **Sonny Cohn (Mrs. Norman)**
> **Pesses Company**
> **Southfield, Michigan**

CHOCOLATE CAKE WITH CHOCOLATE MOCHA FROSTING
(PARVE)

Preparation Time: 10 to 15 minutes
Cooking Time: 30 to 35 minutes
Oven Temperature: 350°

Serves: 15 to 18
Prepare Ahead
Freeze

Cake
¾ c. parve margarine
2 c. sugar
3 eggs
1 tsp. vanilla
½ c. cocoa
1 tsp. soda dissolved in 1 tbsp. water
2 c. flour with a pinch of salt
1 c. cold coffee

Frosting
¼ c. parve margarine
¼ c. cocoa
¼ c. coffee
1 tsp. salt
2 c. confectioners sugar
1 tsp. vanilla

Cake   Sift flour and salt. Put margarine and sugar in mixer and beat until well mixed. Add eggs one at a time and mix until blended. Add vanilla and cocoa and mix well. Add soda which has been mixed with water. Add flour and salt alternately with cold coffee. Turn into 2 greased, lightly floured 9″ pans or one 9″ x 13″ x 2″ pan. Bake in moderate oven (350°) 30 to 35 minutes or until toothpick comes clean when put in center of cake.

Frosting   Allow margarine and coffee to come to room temperature. Sift together sugar, cocoa and salt. Combine all ingredients and beat until smooth.

Allow cake to cool before frosting.

"This is a rich tasting parve cake with beautiful color."

Anne Mervis (Mrs. Samuel B.)
Mervis Industries
Danville, Illinois

PLUM CAKE

Preparation Time: ½ hour
Cooking Time: 1 hour
Oven Temperature: 400°

Serves: 12 to 16
Prepare Ahead

Crust
2 c. all purpose flour
½ tsp. salt
½ tsp. baking powder
1 tbsp. sugar
1½ sticks butter (⅜ lb.) or ¼ lb. butter & ¼ c. shortening
2 egg yolks
2 tbsp. cream
2 tbsp. whiskey

Filling
*3 lb. prune plums (seeded and cut into quarters)
½ to ¾ c. sugar
1 tsp. cinnamon
¼ to ½ c. crushed corn flake crumbs

*Fresh sliced peaches or fresh blueberries may be used instead of plums

Crust   Sift dry ingredients. Add butter (and shortening), then egg yolks beaten with cream and whiskey. Press dough into a spring form pan on bottom and up sides of pan.

Filling   Sprinkle approximately ¼ c. of sugar over bottom of crust. Also sprinkle crushed corn flake crumbs over bottom. Mix sugar with cinnamon and blend into cut up plums. Fill crust with plum mixture. Dot with butter and sprinkle with any sugar left over. Bake one hour at 400°.

"An old family favorite."

Rae Alice Cohen
(Mrs. Bernard W.)
Central Metals Co.
Atlanta, Georgia

SHERRY NUT CAKE

Preparation Time: 45 minutes (including baking time)
Cooking Time: 30 to 35 minutes
Oven Temperature: 350°

Serves: 8 to 12
Prepare Ahead
Freeze

1½ c. flour	**6 tbsp. cooking oil**
1 c. sugar	**1 tsp. vanilla**
½ tsp. salt	**1 c. chopped walnuts**
2 tsp. baking powder	**½ c. water**
2 tsp. nutmeg	**½ c. creme sherry**

Sift dry ingredients together into mixing bowl. Make hole in center and pour in liquid ingredients. Mix well with wire whip. Stir in nuts. Turn into lightly greased 8″ square or 7″ x 10″ rectangular pan and bake in 350° oven for 30 to 35 minutes. May be served with whipped cream or ice cream topped with chopped nuts — or ice with cream cheese icing.

"This is a rich, heavy cake with a moist texture."

Kay Stillman (Mrs. Mike)
Luria Brothers & Co., Inc.
Pueblo, Colorado

RAW APPLE CAKE

Preparation Time: 10 to 15 minutes (not counting apples standing 30 minutes)
Cooking Time: 25 to 30 minutes
Oven Temperature: 350°

Serves: 9
Prepare Ahead
Freeze

2 c. diced apples	**1 tsp. baking soda**
1 c. sugar	**1 tsp. cinnamon**
¼ c. salad oil	**¼ tsp. salt**
1 egg, beaten	**½ c. nuts**
1 c. flour	**1 tsp. vanilla**

Pour sugar over the apples and let stand 30 minutes to draw the juice. Add the oil and beaten egg. Stir the flour with the soda, cinnamon and salt and add to this mixture. Add nuts and vanilla. Pour into greased and floured 8" x 8" x 2" pan. Bake 25 to 30 minutes in 350° oven. Serve warm with whipped cream or sprinkle with powdered sugar.

"Very moist and great with coffee."

Betty Jackson (Mrs. Steven)
Hyman-Michaels
Duluth, Minnesota

CHEESECAKE I

Preparation Time: 15 minutes   *Serves: 8 to 12*
Cooking Time: 1 hour   *Prepare Ahead*
Oven Temperature: 350°   *Freeze*

Crust
1 c. zweiback, crushed
¼ c. sugar (granulated)
¼ c. butter
1 tsp. cinnamon

Cake
1½ lb. cream cheese
4 eggs
⅛ tsp. salt
1 tsp. lemon juice
½ pt. (1 c.) sour cream
1 tsp. vanilla
1 c. sugar (granulated)

Mix together the crust ingredients and press into 9½" spring form pan. Blend together the cream cheese, salt, lemon juice, sour cream, vanilla and sugar. Add to this the eggs, one at a time, blending well. Pour this mixture into the shell. Bake at 350° for 1 hour. Turn oven off, open door and allow to sit in oven and cool for 1 hour. Refrigerate.

"Super rich cheese cake — delicious with or without fruit topping."

Dan D. Shaw
The Scott Equipment Co.
North Branford, Connecticut

CHEESECAKE II

Preparation Time: 2 hours
Cooking Time: 75 minutes

Serves: 12
Prepare Ahead
Freeze

Crust
1 c. sifted all purpose
   flour
¼ c. sugar
1 tsp. grated lemon rind
pinch vanilla bean (inside
   pulp)
1 egg yolk
¼ c. butter

Filling
2½ lbs. cream cheese
1¾ c. sugar
3 tbsp. flour
1½ tsp. grated orange rind
1½ tsp. grated lemon rind
¼ tsp. vanilla extract
5 eggs
2 egg yolks
½ c. heavy cream

Crust Combine flour, sugar, lemon rind and vanilla. Make a well in center and add egg yolk and butter. Work together quickly with hands until well blended. Wrap in wax paper, chill thoroughly in refrigerator for about an hour. Roll out ⅛" thick and place over oiled bottom of 9" spring form cake pan. Trim off excess dough. Bake in hot oven (400°) for 20 minutes. Cool.

Filling Combine cheese, sugar, flour, grated orange and lemon rind and vanilla. Add eggs and egg yolks, one at a time, stirring lightly after each addition. Stir in cream.

Butter sides of cake form and place over base. Roll remaining dough from crust ⅛" thick and cut to fit sides of the oiled pan. Fill with cheese mixture. Bake in very hot oven (550°) 12 to 15 minutes. Reduce temperature to slow (200°) and continue baking one hour. Cool before cutting.

"Mouth-watering, old-fashioned cheesecake; for non-dieters."

Barbara Lazarus (Mrs. David)
Diversified Metals Corp.
St. Louis, Missouri

CHEESE CAKE WITH ENGLISH WALNUT CRUST

DESSERTS

Preparation Time: 15 minutes
Cooking Time: 50 to 60 minutes
Oven Temperature: 375°

Serves: 12 to 15
Prepare Ahead
Freeze

Crust
2 c. + 2 tbsp. graham
cracker crumbs
½ c. + 1 tbsp. butter
1½ c. chopped English
walnuts

Cake
3-8 oz. pkg. softened cream
cheese
1 c. sugar
3 tsp. vanilla
4 eggs
1 c. sour cream

Crust Melt ½ c. butter and mix with 2 c. graham cracker crumbs. Add 1½ c. chopped nuts and mix well. Take 1 tbsp. cold butter and grease all sides of spring form. Take 2 tbsp. of plain graham cracker crumbs and dust the greased sides. Press cracker and nut mixture to bottom of spring form. Set aside.

Cake Cream sugar and cream cheese together until very well blended and fluffy. Add 3 tsp. vanilla that have been beaten with 4 eggs. Add to cheese mixture and blend well. Fold in sour cream and blend. Pour into graham cracker nut crust.

Bake in pre-heated 375° oven for 50 to 60 minutes. Turn off heat but leave cake in oven for another 10 minutes. (Since ovens vary, so will baking time. Watch closely the first time you make recipe.) Test for doneness by inserting a toothpick. Cool cake. The topping for cake can be any canned fruit pie filling. During season, add a cup of fresh fruit to canned topping. Cake freezes well but cake should be served at room temperature.

"This is the most delicious cake. Creamy — and very easy to make and bake."

Miriam Blue (Mrs. George)
Louisville Scrap Material Co.
Louisville, Kentucky

145

CHEESE PIE

Preparation Time: 30 minutes
Cooking Time: 30 minutes
Oven Temperature: 350°

Serves: 10
Prepare Ahead

Crust
1¼ c. graham cracker
   crumbs
¼ c. sugar
¼ c. melted butter or
   margarine

Filling
4 3 oz. pkg. cream cheese
⅔ c. sugar
2 eggs
2 tsp. vanilla
1 c. sour cream
2 tbsp. sugar
1 tsp. vanilla

Crust Combine graham cracker crumbs, sugar and butter. Press into 9 inch pie pan. (Bottom and sides) Bake in 350° oven for 7 minutes. Cool.

Filling In blender, combine cream cheese, ⅔ c. sugar, eggs and 1 tsp. vanilla. Blend until smooth. Pour into pie shell and bake in 350° oven for 20 minutes. Cool. Combine sour cream, 2 tbsp. sugar and 1 tsp. vanilla. Put sour cream mixture onto pie and allow to set for 1 hour. Refrigerate at least 5 hours.

"Very rich but worth it. One of the best."

Eunice Benchell (Mrs. Ernest J.)
Willoughby Iron & Waste
   Materials Co.
Willoughby, Ohio

GRAND MARNIER SAUCE

Preparation Time: 45 to 60 minutes   *Serves: 8*

5 egg yolks   **1 c. whipping cream**
1 c. fine sugar   **¾ c. Grand Marnier**

Put egg yolks in top of double boiler, then beat with a whisk until well mixed. Add the sugar gradually, beating constantly until dissolved. Add the Grand Marnier slowly, beating constantly. Then place over hot, but not boiling, water. Cook for about 3 minutes or until thickened and of lightly whipped cream consistency, beating all the time. Remove from heat and beat for 1 minute longer. Then set on top of double boiler in a bowl of ice. Beat with whisk until cold. Fold in whipping cream carefully until well blended.

"Serve over strawberries and it is out of this world."

Sharlene Pass (Mrs. Barry)
Levin and Sons
Ft. Wayne, Indiana 46806

CREAMY FRUIT DELIGHT

Preparation Time: 45 to 60 minutes   *Serves: 10 to 12*
                                      Prepare Ahead

1¾ c. cold milk   **1 c. thawed Cool Whip***
1 tbsp. orange liqueur   **6 c. fresh fruits**
1-4 oz. pkg. Instant Jello
  vanilla pudding   ***if desired, 1 more c. for use**
                                 on top

Pour milk and liqueur into a bowl adding pudding. Mix. Beat slowly with hand beater 1 minute. Fold in Cool Whip. Arrange ½ of cut-up fresh fruit in bowl. Cover with pudding mix; cover pudding mix with remaining fresh fruit. If desired, top with Cool Whip. Refrigerate 2 to 3 hours.

"Excellent dessert which can be made with various fresh fruits."

Natalie Blum (Mrs. Frank)
Billiton Metals & Ores Inc. U.S.A.
New York, New York

FRUIT GRANTINEE (GRATIN DES FRUITS)

Preparation Time: 30 minutes   *Serves: 6*
Cooking Time: 10 minutes

4 c. assorted fruits   **4 oz. liqueur (Grand**
4 egg yolks   **Marnier, Kirschwasser,**
4 tbsp. sugar   **Pineau des Charentes)**
4 oz. white wine

Clean, pit and cut fruit into small pieces. Suggested fruits are strawberries, orange sections, cherries, peaches. Arrange fruit in ovenproof au gratin dish.

Combine remaining ingredients in metal mixing bowl. Cook mixture in metal bowl over low direct heat (gas stove is preferable). Beat mixture constantly with a wire whisk and cook very slowly. If yolks cook too quickly you will get a scrambled egg look. Cooked slowly the mixture will puff dramatically, steam slightly and become stiff like whipped cream. Mixture is called a sabayon.

Pour sabayon over the fruit and place dish under pre-heated broiler for 10 minutes until slightly browned. Serve immediately.

"A delightful fresh fruit dessert with sabayon sauce."

Lillian Marley (Mrs. Harry)
Marley's
Syracuse, New York

ZABAGLIONE WITH FRUIT

Preparation Time: 15 minutes   *Serves: 4*
Cooking Time: 10 minutes

5 egg yolks   **1½ c. hulled fresh**
½ c. sugar   **strawberries or 1½ c.**
⅓ c. Marsala Wine   **fresh mixed fruit**

Divide fresh fruit among 4 dessert glasses. In top of double boiler, beat egg yolks with wire beater until foamy. Add sugar and continue to beat. Add wine, but do not stop beating when adding wine. Continue to beat until it begins to thicken and is fluffy. Pour into fruit filled dessert glasses and serve at once. (Zabaglione separates if left standing.)

"A warm sweet Italian dessert, sometimes served as a beverage without using the fruit."

Susan Moss (Mrs. Stanton A.)
Stanton A. Moss Inc.
Bryn Mawr, Pennsylvania

MIGHTY MOUSSE

Preparation Time: 30 minutes
Cooking Time: 10 minutes

Serves: 6 to 8
Prepare Ahead

1 pkg. (6 oz.) semi-sweet chocolate chips
2 tsp. instant coffee granules
½ c. sugar

2 tbsp. coffee liqueur (i.e., Kahlua)
½ tsp. vanilla extract
3 eggs, separated
whipped cream, optional

In medium saucepan, over low heat, add chocolate chips, coffee granules, liqueur and ¼ c. sugar. Stir constantly until chocolate is melted and sugar is dissolved. Remove from heat and beat until smooth with wooden spoon. Cool. Add vanilla, then egg yolks one at a time to chocolate mixture; beat well after each egg yolk. Beat egg whites to soft peak stage, then add remaining ¼ c. sugar a tablespoon at a time until stiff peak stage. Incorporate some of egg whites into chocolate mixture; then add chocolate to beaten egg whites, folding gently until well combined. Spoon into individual porcelain souffle cups or demitasse cups. Chill thoroughly for 3 to 4 hours. Garnish, if desired, with whipped cream flavored with Kahlua and chocolate shavings.

"This is a creamy-smooth, rich mocha-chocolate mousse."

Rosalyn C. Richman (Mrs. David)
S.D. Richman Sons, Inc.
Philadelphia, Pennsylvania

149

CHOCOLATE MOUSSE I

Preparation Time: 30 minutes   *Serves: 12*
Cooking Time: 10 minutes   *Prepare Ahead*
                                        Freeze

12 oz. semi-sweet   **¼ tsp. instant coffee**
  chocolate chips   **granules (optional)**
¾ c. sugar   **1 tsp. vanilla**
¼ c. sherry or Kahlua   **¼ tsp. almond extract**
4 large eggs, separated   **16 oz. whipping cream**

Melt chocolate, sugar, coffee and liqueur in top of double boiler or microwave until smooth. Add gradually to beaten egg yolks. Allow to cool. Beat egg whites until stiff and fold in chocolate mixture. Beat whipping cream and fold into mixture. Pour into individual ramekins and allow to set. Sprinkle with chocolate sprinkles. Or, line spring form mold with lady fingers and pour mixture into it. Unmold, decorate with whipped cream and serve.

"An elegant dessert for the chocolate lover."

Eleanor Neiden
Neiden Iron & Metal Co.
Lincoln, Nebraska

CHOCOLATE MOUSSE II

Preparation Time: 10 minutes   *Serves: 4 to 6*
                                        Prepare Ahead

1 c. semi-sweet chocolate   **4 eggs, separated**
  bits   **2 tbsp. dark rum**
5 tbsp. boiling water

Put chocolate in the blender and blend at high speed for 6 seconds. Add water and blend 10 seconds more. Add yolks and rum. Blend until smooth. Fold mixture into stiffly beaten egg whites. Serve with whipped cream or any non-dairy whipped topping and shaved chocolate.

"The beauty of this recipe is that it can even be served for Passover."

Diane Krentzman (Mrs. Stephen)
Joe Krentzman & Son
Lewistown, Pennsylvania

LAYERED CHOCOLATE REFRIGERATOR LOAF

Preparation Time: 30 minutes

Serves: 8 to 10 (Recipe can be tripled. Use 9" x 13" pan.) Prepare Ahead

24 large marshmallows or 2½ c. of miniatures
3 squares (1 oz.) unsweetened chocolate
¾ c. milk
1 tsp. vanilla extract
½ tsp. almond extract
dash salt
1 c. heavy cream, whipped, or 2 c. prepared topping (Cool Whip)
2 pkg. lady fingers
2 or 3 tbsp. (or more) brandy

Melt chocolate and marshmallows over medium heat; add milk. Stir in vanilla and almond extracts; add salt. Chill until thickened. Fold in cream. Set aside. Sprinkle lady fingers with brandy. Line bottom and side of 9" x 5" x 3" loaf pan with ⅓ cream mixture. Layer lady fingers with split sides up. Repeat layers twice. Cover and chill 12 hours or overnight. Unmold. Garnish if desired.

"Scrumptious and no eggs."

Denise Luntz (Mrs. William)
Luntz Corporation
Canton, Ohio

CHOCOLATE ECLAIRS

Preparation Time: 1½ hours
Cooking Time: 35 minutes
Oven Temperature: 400° for 10 minutes
and 350° for 25 minutes

Serves: 10 to 12
Prepare Ahead
Freeze

Shells
¼ lb. butter
1 c. boiling water
1 c. flour
½ tsp. salt
4 eggs

Filling
1⅓ c. sugar
2 c. water
10 tbsp. flour
5 eggs, beaten
½ tsp. salt
2 tsp. vanilla
2 c. evaporated milk

Frosting
½ c. butter
1 egg
½ c. cocoa
¼ tsp. salt
4 c. powdered sugar
1 tsp. vanilla
⅓ c. milk

Shells Add ¼ lb. butter to boiling water; stir to melt butter. Add flour and salt all at once. Cook, stirring vigorously until mixture is smooth and forms a soft ball that doesn't separate. Cool slightly and add 4 eggs one at a time. Beat vigorously after each egg is added. Squeeze through a pastry bag onto greased cookie sheets, ½ to 1 inch wide and 3 inches long. Allow room for spreading. Bake for 10 minutes in preheated 400° oven; reduce oven to 350° and continue baking for 25 minutes. Cool shells; split and add cooled filling.

Filling Combine flour, sugar and salt in saucepan. Add milk and water gradually, beating constantly until smooth. Cook 10 minutes over low heat stirring constantly. Pour over eggs. Return to sauce pan and cook 2 minutes or until thick, stirrir ⁻tantly. Cool and add vanilla.

Frosting   Blend butter, egg, cocoa and salt. Add sugar alternately with milk and vanilla. Mix until smooth. Frost tops of eclairs. Chill. Will frost about 24 eclairs.

Mrs. Victor Vollhardt
Frankel Iron & Metal Co.
Fontana, California

STRAWBERRY PRETZEL DESSERT

Cooking Time: 10 minutes
Oven Temperature: 350°

Serves: 8 to 10
Prepare Ahead (1 day)

2⅔ c. ground pretzels
1½ sticks melted butter
1-8 oz. pkg. cream cheese
1 c. sugar

1 pkg. Dream Whip
2 pkg. strawberry Jello
2 pkg. frozen strawberries

Mix ground pretzels with melted butter and spread in 9" x 12" or 9" x 13" pan. Bake 10 minutes in 350° oven. Set aside to cool. Mix cream cheese and sugar. Prepare Dream Whip and fold into cream cheese mixture. Spread over pretzel crust and set aside. Mix strawberry Jello with 2 c. water. Stir in frozen strawberries and allow mixture to set slightly. Spread strawberry mixture over cheese mixture and refrigerate.

"Makes a delicious dessert."

Lois Phillips (Mrs. Fred)
Phillips Iron & Supply Co.
St. Cloud, Minnesota

ALASKAN TRIFLE

Cooking Time: 35 minutes
Oven Temperature: 350°

Serves: 8 to 10
Prepare Ahead
  (must be a day
  ahead)
Freeze

Cake
1⅓ c. flour
1 c. sugar
3 tbsp. unsweetened cocoa
½ tsp. salt
½ tsp. vanilla
1 egg
⅓ c. cooking oil
½ tsp. baking soda
¾ c. water

Filling
1 pkg. vanilla pudding
¾ c. apricot preserves
1 c. whipping cream
1 tbsp. sugar
¼ c. sherry
milk (according to
  directions on
  pudding mix)

Cake In small mixing bowl, stir together flour, sugar, cocoa, soda and salt. Add egg, oil, water and vanilla. Blend at low speed, then beat two minutes at medium speed. Bake in 8″ x 8″ pan, 350° for 35 minutes.

Filling In small pan prepare package of vanilla pudding according to instructions; reduce milk to 1¾ c.; stir sherry into the cooked pudding and cover until it cools (about one hour).

To Assemble Slit cake horizontally into two layers. Spread the bottom layer with apricot preserves and replace top of cake. (The cake can be made the day before.) Line a 2½ qt. decorative bowl with plastic wrap. Spread ½ c. of vanilla filling in bottom of bowl. Cut the cake into one inch squares. Place ⅓ of cake squares on top of filling in bowl. Spoon in another

½ c. filling and repeat layers. Cover all with plastic wrap and press gently and chill. Invert onto plate and remove wrap. Decorate with sweetened whipped cream and garnish with nuts.

"Very elegant and unusual dessert."

Dorothy Tabakin (Mrs. Gilbert)
Gilbert Iron & Metal Co.
Steubenville, Ohio

NO EGG COFFEE CAKE

Preparation Time: 10 minutes   *Freeze*
Cooking Time: 1 hour
Oven Temperature: 325°

Cake
¾ c. butter
1½ c. sugar
1½ tsp. vanilla
1½ c. sour cream
3 c. flour
1½ tsp. baking powder
1½ tsp. baking soda
½ tsp. salt
½ c. beer

Topping
⅔ c. chopped walnuts
½ c. sugar
1½ tsp. cinnamon

Cream butter and sugar. Add rest of ingredients. Beat together and pour ⅓ of cake batter into a 10″ greased and floured tube pan. Cover with ⅓ topping mixture. Repeat twice.

Joan P. Millens (Mrs. Barney)
B. Millens Sons, Inc.
Kingston, New York

SOUR CREAM COFFEE CAKE

Cooking Time: 40 minutes　　　*Serves: 6*
Oven Temperature: 350°　　　*Prepare Ahead*
　　　　　　　　　　　　　　Freeze

Cake
½ pt. sour cream
¼ c. butter or margarine
2 c. cake flour
2 eggs
1 tsp. baking soda
1 tsp. baking powder
1 c. sugar
1 tsp. vanilla

Filling
½ c. chopped walnuts
⅓ c. brown sugar
⅓ c. white sugar
1 tsp. cinnamon

Mix filling ingredients and set aside. Cream butter, sugar and eggs until light. Sift together flour, baking powder and baking soda. Add flour mixture, sour cream and vanilla to egg mixture alternately while beating at medium speed. Beat until well blended. Cake batter will be heavy so spoon, don't pour, ½ cake mixture into a greased and lightly floured 9″ x 9″ square baking pan; even out batter with spoon. Sprinkle ½ filling mixture over cake batter. Add remaining cake batter and top with other half of filling; even out batter. Bake for 40 minutes or until a toothpick inserted in center of cake comes out clean, at 350°.

Isabelle Daniels (Mrs. Robert)
K & D Salvage
Bakersfield, California

SCRUMPTIOUS STRUDEL

Preparation Time: 40 minutes
Cooking Time: 35 minutes
Oven Temperature: 450° and 350°

Serves: 4 rolls
Prepare Ahead
Freeze

Batter
½ lb. butter or margarine
½ pt. sour cream
2 c. sifted all purpose
   flour
¼ tsp. almond flavoring

Filling
1 lb. jar apricot preserves
1 c. chopped coconut
1 c. chopped nuts
¾ c. raisins

Cut butter or margarine into flour with two forks. Add sour cream and almond flavoring. Form mixture into ball and refrigerate overnight. When ready to use, divide dough into four parts. Roll ¼ of dough at a time on floured board. Keep the rest of dough in refrigerator until ready to use. Mix together all ingredients for filling. Spread filling on dough and roll as for a jelly roll. Bake on floured jelly roll pan for 10 minutes in 450° oven; then reduce temperature to 350° and bake for an additional 25 minutes or until lightly brown. Remove strudel from pan when cold and cut into desired size pieces.

"Puff pastry and delicious filling make this a yummy concoction."

Sara Dinberg (Mrs. Walter)
Southern Foundry & Supply
Chattanooga, Tennessee

LONG COFFEE CAKE

Cooking Time: 1 hour
Oven Temperature: 350°

Batter
4 eggs
1 tsp. vanilla
1 tbsp. butter extract
1 pkg. instant vanilla
   pudding
1 pkg. Duncan Hines
   Deluxe Yellow Cake
   Mix
¾ c. oil
¾ c. water
1 pkg. Dream Whip

Filling
¼ c. sugar
2 tsp. cinnamon
2 tsp. chopped nuts

Frosting
¾ c. sugar
1½ tbsp. milk
1 tsp. butter extract
1 tsp. vanilla

Mix all batter ingredients together and beat for 7 minutes. Grease (Spry) and flour angel food cake pan. Pour ¾ of mixture into pan. Sprinkle with mixture of filling ingredients. Cover with remaining batter; swirl with knife; bake in preheated 350° oven for 1 hour or more. Cool 10 minutes and remove cake from pan. Allow cake to finish cooling. Prepare glaze from frosting ingredients and drizzle over cake.

Jan Davis (Mrs. Yale)
West End Iron & Metal Corp.
Duluth, Minnesota

RUGGELACH

Preparation Time: 45 minutes
Cooking Time: 20 minutes
Oven Temperature: 375°

Serves: 48
*   cookies*
Prepare Ahead
Freeze

apricot jam
1 pkg. yeast
3 egg yolks
½ lb. butter, melted
½ pt. sour cream

3 c. flour
1 c. sugar
1 tsp. cinnamon
optional — add finely
   chopped walnuts to dough

Dissolve yeast in ¼ c. warm water. Mix flour, yeast and melted butter. Add egg yolks and sour cream. Refrigerate overnight. Divide dough into 6 pieces. Mix sugar and cinnamon and sprinkle mixture onto pastry cloth or board. Roll one piece of dough at a time in cinnamon-sugar mixture, into a 8" or 9" circle. Cut like a pizza into 8 wedges. Put a tiny dab of apricot jam at wide edge — roll down to pointed edge. Place on greased cookie sheet. Continue until all pieces are prepared. Bake in 375° oven for 20 minutes.

"They look like and taste like what mama used to make."

Mrs. Florence Goldberg
M. Pashelinsky & Sons, Inc.
Jersey City, New Jersey

IRISH TEA BRACK

Preparation Time: 10 to 15 minutes
Cooking Time: 1½ hours
Oven Temperature: 300°

Serves: 8 to 12
per loaf
Prepare Ahead
Freeze

1 lb. golden raisins (3 c.)
1 lb. raisins (reg.) (3 c.)
1 lb. brown sugar (2⅓ c.)
3 c. milkless tea, or
mixture of half tea and
half Irish Whiskey

1 lb. flour (3 c.)
3 eggs, beaten
3 level tsp. baking powder
3 tsp. mixed spice (optional)

Soak the fruit and sugar in tea overnight. Next day add alternately the flour and eggs. Add baking powder and mixed spice. Turn into three greased loaf pans 8" x 4" x 3" and bake for 1½ hours in 300° oven. When cool, brush top with melted honey for a fine glaze. Slice thin and serve buttered or with cream cheese.

"Moist and not too sweet — keeps very well."

Eileen Huff (Mrs. Richard M.)
Huff's Iron & Metal Co., Inc.
Fort Mill, South Carolina

APRICOT STRUDEL

Preparation Time: 30 minutes on 2 different days (may take longer on second day)
Cooking Time: 25 to 30 minutes
Oven Temperature: 350°

Serves: 72 slices
Prepare Ahead
Freeze

2½ c. flour
1 tsp. baking powder (scant)
1 c. sour cream
½ lb. butter (can use ¼ lb. butter and ¼ lb. margarine)

2 egg yolks
apricot preserves
chopped walnuts
white raisins
coconut, if desired
cinnamon
sugar

Crumble butter, flour and baking powder together. Beat egg yolks into sour cream. Add to flour mixture. Mix thoroughly. Shape into ball. Refrigerate overnight. Cut into 6 or more pieces. Roll each piece on floured board into oblong shapes. Spread each oblong shape with apricot preserves, chopped walnuts, white raisins and coconut (if you desire). Roll into 6 long logs. Put on slightly greased cookie sheet with open side down. Sprinkle with cinnamon and sugar. Bake in 350° oven about 25 to 30 minutes or until brown. When cool, slice into one inch slices.

"Elegantly served with powdered sugar on top and placed into small individual paper cups."

Doris Gordon (Mrs. Bernard)
Gordon Waste Co.
Columbia, Pennsylvania

LEMON CHEESE SQUARES

Preparation Time: 45 minutes　　　*Serves: 20 to 24*
Cooking Time: 10 to 15 minutes　　*Prepare Ahead*
Oven Temperature: 375°

Crust
2 c. flour
1 stick butter
1 stick margarine
2 tbsp. confectioners
   sugar

Filling #1
2-8 oz. pkg. cream cheese
2 c. confectioners sugar
1-8 oz. container Cool
   Whip

Filling #2
2 pkg. Royal lemon pudding
1 can or pkg. flaked coconut

Crust　Combine flour, butter, margarine and confectioners sugar. Pat into a 9" x 13" glass pan. Bake at 375° 10 to 15 minutes. Set aside to cool.

Filling #1　Beat cream cheese and confectioners sugar until smooth. Fold in Cool Whip and spread mixture over baked crust.

Filling #2　Cook pudding according to directions. Cool and spread over cheese mixture. Sprinkle top with coconut. Chill several hours and cut into squares to serve.

"A refreshing and delicious dessert, pleasing to the palate as well as the eye."

**Ruth Zudekoff (Mrs. Sherman)
United Scrap Iron & Metal Co.,
   Inc.
New Haven, Connecticut**

LEBKUCHEN

Preparation Time: 30 minutes
Cooking Time: 30 minutes
Oven Temperature: 375°

Serves: 24
Prepare Ahead
Freeze

4 whole eggs
1 c. sugar
1 c. molasses (Grandma's Brand)
2 cakes sweet chocolate, melted
1 tsp. cinnamon
1 tsp allspice

1 tsp. cloves
2 c. flour
1 tsp. baking powder
2 c. nuts
2 c. dates
powdered sugar (optional)

Mix eggs and sugar and beat until very light. Add molasses, melted chocolate and spices. Add flour and baking powder. Add nuts and dates. Spread in 9" x 13" pan which has been greased and dusted with flour. Bake for 30 minutes at 375°. Cut into squares. Finish by dusting tops with powdered sugar. Powdered sugar glaze may be used if desired.

"A fruit and nut cake."

Lynne Lipsitz
M. Lipsitz & Co., Inc.
Waco, Texas

CHOCOLATE CHEESE CUPS

Preparation Time: 1½ hours
Cooking Time: 20 minutes
Oven Temperature: 300°

Serves: 9 dozen
bite size
Prepare Ahead
Freeze

3 c. flour
½ c. cocoa
2 c. sugar
2 tsp. baking soda
1 tsp. salt
2 c. water

⅔ c. cooking oil
2 tbsp. vinegar
24 oz. cream cheese
3 beaten eggs
1 c. sugar
18 oz. chocolate chips

Sift together flour, cocoa, 2 c. sugar, baking soda and salt in mix-master bowl. Add water, oil, vinegar. Beat all together. Fill muffin tins half full with this mixture. Then beat cream cheese, eggs, 1 c. sugar in mix-master and stir in chocolate chips. Top the half filled tins with the cheese topping — leaving room as cups will rise. Bake in 350° oven for 20 minutes.

"Excellent served with other sweets on dessert trays."

Paula Simon (Mrs. Joseph)
Alma Iron & Metal Co., Inc.
Alma, Michigan

PECAN TARTS

Preparation Time: 15 minutes
Cooking Time: 15 minutes
Oven Temperature: 400°

Serves: 10 to 15
Prepare Ahead
Freeze

Tart Shell
½ c. margarine
½ c. sugar
2 egg yolks
1 tsp. almond extract
2 c. sifted flour

Filling
½ c. margarine
⅓ c. dark corn syrup
1 c. confectioners sugar
1 c. chopped pecans

Tart Shell   Mix margarine, sugar, egg yolks and almond extract together well. Stir in flour. Press evenly into fluted tart shells. Bake at 400° 8 to 10 minutes. Makes 10 3-inch or 15 1½-inch fluted tart shells.

Filling   Bring margarine, corn syrup and sugar to boil. Stir in 1 cup chopped pecans. Spoon into baked shells. Top with pecan halves. Bake at 350° for 5 minutes.

"Perfect for parties — also is kosher and parve."

Happy Kramer (Mrs. Norman)
MAC Corporation
Grand Prairie, Texas

163

TEA TIME TARTS

Preparation Time: 15 minutes
Cooking Time: 30 to 35 minutes
Oven Temperature: 375°

Serves: 24
Prepare Ahead
Freeze

Pastry
1 small pkg. cream cheese
1 c. flour
1 stick sweet margarine
   or butter

Filling
1 c. brown sugar
1 tsp. vanilla
1 c. walnuts, chopped fine
   (can also use pecans or ½
   c. of each)
1 egg
1 tbsp. soft butter
pinch of salt
powdered sugar

Blend pastry ingredients and roll into 24 balls. Put in refrigerator to chill for about one hour. When cool, press into 24 1" muffin tins to form a shell. Fill center of shell with filling ingredients that have been blended together. Bake at 375° for 30 to 35 minutes. Cook and sprinkle with powdered sugar on top.

"A delectable miniature cupcake."

Anne Turkel (Mrs. Harry)
Atlantic Metal Traders, Inc.
Yonkers, New York

SOFT CHOCOLATE CHIP COOKIES

Preparation Time: 15 to 20 minutes
Cooking Time: 10 to 12 minutes
Oven Temperature: 400°

Serves: 2 dozen
   cookies
Prepare Ahead
Freeze

½ c. butter
2 eggs
1½ c. sugar
½ tsp. vanilla
3 c. sifted flour
½ tsp. baking powder

½ tsp. baking soda
1 c. sour cream
1½ c. semi-sweet chocolate
   chips, lightly dredged in
   flour
cinnamon-sugar mixture

Sift together flour, baking powder and baking soda. Cream butter and sugar. Add eggs one at a time to butter mixture; add vanilla and beat until mixture is light and fluffy. Alternate adding flour mixture and sour cream to butter mixture, starting and ending with the flour. Fold in chocolate chips. Drop mixture by large tablespoons (silverware type) onto cookie sheet and sprinkle with cinnamon-sugar mixture. Important: Cookies will not be soft if made too small. Bake in 400° oven 10 to 12 minutes or until golden brown on bottom.

"Large, soft butter chocolate chips cookies."

Regina Feldman-Goldstein
(Mrs. Jeffrey)
Alter Company
Davenport, Iowa

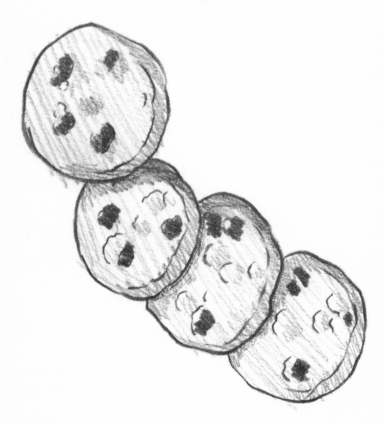

CHOCOLATE SQUARES

Preparation Time: 15 minutes   *Serves: 20*
Cooking Time: 30 minutes   *Prepare Ahead*
Oven Temperature: 350°   *Freeze*

Cake
2 c. flour
2 c. sugar
1 tsp. baking soda
1 tsp. cinnamon
1 c. butter
1 c. water
4 tbsp. cocoa
2 eggs
1 tsp. vanilla
½ c. buttermilk

Icing
4 tbsp. cocoa
1 stick butter
6 tbsp. milk
1 tsp. vanilla
1 lb. box confectionary
  sugar
1½ c. coarsely chopped nuts

Cake   Sift dry ingredients together. Melt butter in water; add cocoa; stir and bring mixture to a boil. Pour cocoa mixture over dry ingredients and beat with electric mixer. Add 2 eggs, one at a time, mixing well. Add vanilla and buttermilk. Pour into a jelly roll pan and bake at 350° for 25 to 30 minutes.

Icing   Blend all ingredients together. When cake is almost cool spread over cake. Cut cake into squares.

"It tastes like a fudge chocolate brownie."

Betty Glick (Mrs. Morde)
Tri-State Iron & Metal Co.
Texarkana, Arkansas

DOUBLE CHOCOLATE MINT BROWNIES

Preparation Time: 1 hour, 15 minutes
Cooking Time: 25 minutes
Oven Temperature: 350°

Serves: 40
  brownies
Prepare Ahead
Freeze

Batter
1 stick butter (¼ lb.)
1 1 lb. can chocolate
  syrup
1 c. sugar
4 eggs
1 c. flour
1 c. chopped nuts

Frosting
1 stick butter (¼ lb.)
⅓ c. evaporated milk (half
  of small can)
1½ c. sugar
6 oz. chocolate chips
1 tsp. peppermint flavoring

Batter Cream butter and sugar until fluffy. Beat in syrup, then eggs, one at a time. Beat in flour gradually. Fold in chopped nuts. Pour into greased 15" x 10" jelly roll pan. Bake at 350° for 25 minutes. DO NOT OVERBAKE.

Frosting In saucepan, combine butter, sugar and evaporated milk. Boil for one minute. Stir in chocolate chips, heat and stir until melted. Add peppermint flavoring and stir. Frosting will be thin and glossy. Frost brownies immediately and quickly. Decorate with nuts or chocolate sprinkles.

"One bite — you'll crave them!"

Marianna Csizmadia
(Mrs. Frank)
Miller Compressing Co.
Milwaukee, Wisconsin

HEAVENLY HASH BROWNIES

Preparation Time: 40 minutes (cooking   *Freeze*
    time included)
Cooking Time: 28 to 35 minutes
Oven Temperature: 350°

Brownie
2 sticks butter (1 c.)
4 tbsp. cocoa
4 eggs
2 c. sugar
1½ tsp. flour
pinch salt
2 tsp. vanilla

Icing
6 tbsp. butter
¾ c. Pet milk
6 c. powdered sugar (1½
    boxes)
¾ c. cocoa
1 large bag marshmallows

In a saucepan, melt the butter and add cocoa; beat the eggs separately and add sugar; mix with butter and cocoa. Add flour, salt and vanilla and mix well. Pour into greased pan and bake for 28 to 35 minutes (test) in a 350° oven.

While brownies are baking, mix all icing ingredients and heat over a double boiler, stirring constantly. When brownies are done, remove from oven and immediately put marshmallows on hot brownies and pour hot icing mixture over top. Let cool and then cut into squares.

Denise Newman (Mrs. S. Mark)
A. Newman & Company
St. Catharines, Ontario, Canada

A

B

INDEX